THE TRUE STORY OF THE KELLY GANG OF BUSHRANGERS

C.H. CHOMLEY

ETT IMPRINT

Exile Bay

This edition published by ETT Imprint, Exile Bay 2021

First published by Pater & Co, Melbourne 1900

This book is copyright. Apart from any fair dealing for the purposes of private study, research, criticism or review, as permitted under the Copyright Act, no part may be reproduced by any process without written permission. Inquiries should be addressed to the publishers via email to ettimprint@hotmail.com or to:.

ETT IMPRINT
PO Box R1906
Royal Exchange NSW 1225 Australia

Copyright © this edition ETT Imprint 2020

ISBN 978-1-922473-30-1 (ebook)
ISBN 978-1-922473-29-5 (paper)

C over: The Kelly Gang's armour after the Siege of Glenrowan, photograph by Oswald Maddeley 1880

Cover and internal design by Tom Thompson

CONTENTS

1. THE MURDERS ON THE WOMBAT	5
2. FINDING THE BODIES	11
3. THE BUSHRANGERS' COUNTRY	16
4. WHY THE KELLYS "WENT OUT"	22
5. POLICE PREPARATIONS	26
6. MR. NICOLSON IN PURSUIT – THE OUTLAWRY BILL	31
7. THE RAT'S CASTLE FIASCO	37
8. THE OUTLAWS' LOST TO SIGHT	43
9. MR. WYATT AND THE BROKEN WIRES	48
10. THE STICKING-UP OF FAITHFULL'S CREEK	55
11. THE EUROA BANK ROBBERY	62
12. A CHANGE IN THE COMMAND	67
13. THE KELLY GANG AT JERILDERIE	74
14. THE CAMP AT MRS. BYRNE'S	82
15. FRUITLESS EFFORTS	89
16. A CHANGE IN THE PLAN OF CAMPAIGN	96
17. AARON SHERRITT'S DEATH	103
18. THE PRISONERS AT GLENROWAN	109
19. THE ASSAULT UPON THE HOTEL	115
20. FIRE AND FLAMES	119
21. THE LAST OF THE BUSHRANGERS	126

NOTE

While it is not claimed that no errors have crept into the following narrative, the writer, having carefully consulted official documents, newspapers of the time, and other sources of information, believes that he is justified in describing it as a "true story."

Dan Kelly's armour, Ned Kelly's rifle and armour, photographed after the seige at Glenrowan.

1
THE MURDERS ON THE WOMBAT

ON a Sunday afternoon of October, 1878, the little Victorian town of Mansfield was wrapped in its usual quiet and peacefulness, when a horseman riding through the streets attracted the attention of all residents who chanced to be abroad. He seemed utterly weary. His clothes were torn and mud-stained. His pale, horror-stricken face, his whole appearance suggested that he had undergone some terrible experience, and he was making his way to the police-station, where Sub-Inspector Pewtress, an officer just arrived from Melbourne, was in charge.

These things excited curiosity. The man was known to be one Constable McIntyre. But he did not stay to be questioned, and the knot of people who gathered round the doors of the police-station waited anxiously to hear his story.

"They're all killed, sir. The Kellys have murdered them all," were the words with which he greeted his superior officer, and it was some time before he could give a connected account of the experiences he had been through.

Gradually, however, he recovered himself, and made Mr. Pewtress acquainted with the facts.

On Friday morning, October 25, under the orders of Sergeant Kennedy, and accompanied also by Constables Scanlon and Lonigan, he had set out from Mansfield in search of the Kellys — two brothers for whose arrest orders had been issued on various charges, of which more anon. It was believed that they were somewhere in the neighbourhood of Mansfield; but in the mountainous country, heavily forested, sparsely settled, and cut up by valleys and creeks, whose banks were clothed in almost impenetrable scrub, there seemed but a faint chance of discovering and arresting them. The party looked forward to spending some considerable time in the wilds. All men were mounted. They were furnished with provisions for three weeks, and in a nondescript fashion they were armed, each man carrying a revolver, in addition to which they had among them a repeating rifle and a double-barrelled gun.

Early on Friday morning they left the police-station, directing their course into the mountainous country which surrounds Mansfield, itself a picturesquely situated village, nestling among the hills in the north-eastern district of Victoria. Though the object of their expedition was nominally secret, and they had substituted ordinary bush costume for uniform, it was pretty generally known in the township that they were in search of the Kellys, whose horse-stealing exploits, and the alleged attempted murder of a certain Constable Fitzpatrick, had made them notorious in the district.

On Friday evening the police pitched their camp in the Wombat Ranges, on the banks of Stringy Bark Creek, about twenty miles from Mansfield, and not far from a spot reputed to be one of the Kellys' bush haunts. On the Saturday morning Sergeant Kennedy, taking Constable Scanlon with him, patrolled down the creek leaving the other two men in camp, and directing Constable McIntyre to do the cooking for the party. Kennedy and Scanlon were mounted, for though the country is rough in the extreme, no Australian bushman ever thinks of walking where it is possible for a horse to get foothold, or scramble through the trees. Wattle and sassafras scrub clothed the banks of the creek. An open patch of ground, comparatively free from timber, was covered with clumps of bayonet grass six feet high, and beyond was a forest of stringy bark and other gum trees rising above the bracken and undergrowth, and shutting in the view of either side. The police tent was pitched among the bayonet grass, near a huge fallen tree.

Constables Lonigan and McIntyre had little in the camp to occupy them, and spent much of the day in yarning over their chances of capturing the Kellys, while McIntyre amused himself for a time by shooting parrots in the neighbouring forest. At five o'clock the sergeant and Scanlon were still away and the other two were making tea in expectation of their return. McIntyre was putting the billy on the fire. Lonigan stood talking by his side. Suddenly they heard voices calling to them: "Bail up! Hold up your hands!"

Looking round they saw that they were covered by the guns of four men, who had stolen up to the camp unheard, and evidently intended mischief. McIntyre was unarmed. He had left his revolver in the tent, and resistance being hopeless, he held his arms above his head. Three or four yards from the fire there stood a tree, and Lonigan made a bolt for it, at the same time endeavouring to draw the revolver which he carried slung to his belt. He had scarcely taken a step, however, and had no time to grasp his revolver, before he was fired upon, and fell on his face, crying, "O Christ! I'm shot." He never spoke again, for he had been shot dead by Edward Kelly, and the curtain had risen on a sordid, yet exciting drama, which was to engross the interest of Victoria for years.

When Lonigan fell the four men rushed upon McIntyre, ordering him to keep his hands up, lest he, too, should be armed and show fight. McIntyre obeyed, and stood still. Edward Kelly searched him for firearms, and, finding that he had none, asked him where he had put his revolver. It was in the tent, he told them; and when one of the murderers had secured it, Ned Kelly, the leader, told McIntyre that he might drop his hands and sit down upon a log. Then he turned his attention to Lonigan, and saw that he was dead. "Dear, dear!" he said, "what a pity that man tried to get away! But you're all right."

Thereupon he lit his pipe and looked round to take stock of the camp, questioning McIntyre as to the arms and ammunition the police party possessed, and the whereabout of his mates. The other men took the billy off the fire and invited their prisoner to smoke and take tea with them, while Ned Kelly told him of what he intended to do. Ned's brother, Daniel Kelly, producing a pair of police handcuffs which he had obtained in the tent, proposed that McIntyre should wear them; but, significantly tapping his rifle, Ned remarked, "I have something better than handcuffs here." He added, for McIntyre's benefit, that, should he attempt to escape, he would track him even into Mansfield and shoot him down like a dog.

Meanwhile McIntyre, with the murdered body of his mate before him as a reminder of what further ill might happen, was anxiously awaiting the return of his mates. Kelly questioned him closely as to their movements. Evidently, to McIntyre's surprise, he knew a good deal about the camp and party which was, after all, not surprising, since the sound of the constable's parrot- shooting must have guided Kelly to the spot, allowing him to watch the police, unseen, from the cover of the scrub, and to listen to their conversation before he made his attack. Asked when he expected Scanlon and Kennedy to return, McIntyre said that he had long been waiting for them and believed they must have got bushed. He begged Kelly not to shoot them. Kennedy, he said, was a married man and the father of a family, whom, surely, he could not murder in cold blood. Kelly said he wanted to murder nobody, and would shoot no man who held up his arms. He knew nothing about Kennedy, but believed Scanlon was a "flash − −, that wanted taking down a bit." However, he would not shoot if the men surrendered.

Did he intend to shoot him? McIntyre asked.

"No", said Kelly. "If I had wanted to shoot you, I could have done so half-an-hour ago."

Then, for some time, while his mates appear to have sat apart, or busied themselves in annexing police property, Kelly moralised to McIntyre on the laziness and discredit of great big strapping fellows like himself and the dead Lonigan leading a loafing life in the police force. They should be ashamed of themselves, he said. He added that at first he had believed McIntyre to be Constable Flood, against whom he had a grievance, and that if he had been, they would have roasted him on the fire. Constable Fitzpatrick he alleged to be the cause of the present trouble. He declared that there had been no attack made upon him, and that through the constable's perjury Mrs. Kelly, Ned's mother, was in gaol, and himself and his brother driven into the bush. McIntyre listened, waiting all the time for the sound of horsemen approaching. He had experienced Kelly's cool indifference to taking life, and feared for the fate of his comrades. What was to be done with them? He asked. Would Kelly give his word that they should not be killed?

Prefacing his remarks with the suggestion that the police came out to kill him, which McIntyre denied, saying their intention was only to arrest, Kelly promised mercy, on condition that McIntyre induced Kennedy and Scanlon to surrender and hold up their hands as they reached the camp. In that case, he said, he would handcuff them all night, take their horses and arms, and allow them to depart in the morning. "But you had better be sure you do make them surrender," he added, "otherwise I will shoot you."

Partly satisfied, McIntyre asked if Kelly would promise that the other men should not shoot them. "I won't shoot," said Kelly shortly. "The other men may please themselves." During this conversation one of the men was hidden in the tent, the other two in the scrub, and Kelly was just signalling them to report his arrangement with McIntyre, where there came the sound of horses' hoofs and rustling bushes nearby.

"Hush, lads!" called Kelly in a low voice. "Here they come. Sit down on that log," he whispered sternly to McIntyre, who had risen in his excitement, "or I'll put a hole through you."

"For God's sake don't shoot the men," replied McIntyre, "and I'll get them to surrender." Just as he spoke Kennedy and Scanlon emerged from the scrub into full view in the open ground of the camp. McIntyre ran forward towards Kennedy, asking him to surrender, as the camp was surrounded. The police looked round bewildered, suspecting some practical joke, but almost simultaneously with McIntyre's appeal Kelly and his mates called out, "Bail up! Throw your hands up!"

Scanlon and Kennedy were both brave men. They sprang from their horses, Kennedy attempting to take cover behind his, as he drew his revolver, and Scanlon making for a tree, trying to unsling his rifle while he ran.

Immediately the Kellys began firing, and Scanlon fell with a gun-shot under his arm, and blood spurting from his side, before he could reach the tree, or raise the rifle to his shoulder. It is doubtful whether Kennedy heard McIntyre's repeated entreaty to surrender. At any rate he disregarded it and showed fight; but he, too, fell wounded before he could fire his revolver, and dropped upon his knees.

All this time the bullets had been whistling past McIntyre. "All right, boys, I surrender. Stop it! Stop it!" he heard Kennedy call as he fell. But the firing still went on. Kennedy had released the bridle of his horse, which passed close to McIntyre. Seeing that the case was hopeless, and knowing that if he remained he too would be murdered, quick as thought he leapt on to Kennedy's horse and galloped away through thick scrub.

Dan Kelly was the first to notice his attempted escape. "Shoot that — ——. Shoot that ———," McIntyre heard him call, and several shots followed, while bullets sang close past his ears, but none of them struck him; and soon the sound of firing and voices from the camp died away, as he pushed feverishly on towards Mansfield. It was rough riding through the timber for horse and man.

Bumped against the trees, his body bruised, his face scratched and bleeding, and his clothes torn to pieces by the scrub, McIntyre pressed forward, fearing pursuit, until dusk. Then his horse fell heavily. He mounted again and rode on for a time till his horse gave in; when, believing him to be wounded, the constable took of saddle and bridle, let him go, and running a short distance, concealed himself in a wombat hole, where he made a short memo in his note-book of what had occurred. The notes, which were evidently written under the strain of great fatigue and excitement, McIntyre had some vague notion might be discovered in the future, should the bushrangers come upon his hiding-place and make away with him. It is obvious that unless the bushrangers came upon the man and his notes together, the chance of the latter ever being found in a wombat hole in the vastnesses of the bush was the remotest; but confused thought was natural enough in McIntyre's circumstances. However that be, he wrote as follows:—

> *"Ned Kelly and others stuck us up to-day, when we were disarmed. Lonigan and Scanlon shot. I am hiding in wombat hole until dark. The Lord have mercy upon me.*
> *Scanlon tried to get his gun out."* There the wombat- hole reflections *terminate, but later on he wrote, "I have been travelling all night, and am very weary. Nine a.m., Sunday.—I am now lying on the edge of a creek named Bridges'."*

These entries refer to the following day. After dark, on the night of the murder, McIntyre left his hiding place and made his way on foot through the bush in the direction of Mansfield. Every sound startled him, for he feared the bushrangers were on his track, and progress through the scrub and forest, where huge fallen trees half-hidden in bracken and undergrowth barred the way, was painful and difficult. Resting for a time by the creek where he made his latest entries in the note-book, he pushed on by daylight through almost uninhabited country, meeting no one until he reached the homestead of a settler named M'Coll, about one and a half miles from Mansfield.

There he waited a little while, telling disconnected scraps of his story, after which he continued his sad journey to Mansfield, where he arrived to disturb the sleepy quiet of the township Sunday afternoon with the gruesome tale, which, bit by bit, Inspector Pewtress drew from him.

The Attack on the Police Camp.—

2
FINDING THE BODIES

WHEN McIntyre reached the police-station Sub-inspector Pewtress was lying in bed, ill with cold and influenza. He had arrived in Mansfield from Melbourne, via Benalla, the headquarters of the district police, only the day before, and though he knew that Kennedy and other constables were absent from the town on special duty, he was not aware of its nature. The knowledge of what the police mission had been, and McIntyre's excited account of its disastrous ending, quickly roused the police officer, who forgot for the time that he was ill and left his bed to make immediate arrangements for a search—possibly a rescue—party. Scanlon and Lonigan, McIntyre was sure were dead, but it was possible that Kennedy might be alive. When the news spread through Mansfield it roused the people to a high pitch of horror and excitement, not unmixed with fear, and the wildest pictures were conjured up of the outlaws coming out of the bush to rob and burn the town. Absurd as these fears may seem, it was, after all, only the objectlessness of a murderous attack from the outlaws that made them so. There was scarcely a firearm of any kind in Mansfield, and a determined party of men armed with rifles and revolvers might have done almost as they chose. However, there was no difficulty in finding hardy volunteers ready to venture out into the bush to the scene of the tragedy. The Inspector spoke to some of the leading townspeople, among them Dr. Reynolds, the local medical practitioner, and a party of five volunteers was quickly organised. Two constables, Meehan and Allwood, were at the time on the station. The former Mr. Pewtress despatched with a report from McIntyre and his own notes thereon, to his superior officer, Superintendent Sadleir at Benalla, distant some forty miles from Mansfield. Inspector Pewtress had tried to telegraph, but was unable to get a message over the wires, and accordingly directed Meehan to ride without drawing rein to Broken River, about half-way, and there procure a fresh horse to continue his journey. He should have reached his destination before midnight of that day, but, as showing the excited nervous state in which was endangered in weak heads by the Kelly outrage, it may be mentioned that Meehan, catching a glimpse of some stranger near the Broken River, immediately let his horse go and concealed himself, believing that he was pursued by the bushrangers. As a consequence of his powerful imagination he did not reach his destination until the evening of the following day.

11

Inspector Pewtress, believing that he had sent the news expeditiously, turned his attention to other affairs and acted with the utmost promptitude. In spite of his broken-up condition, Constable McIntyre pluckily insisted upon accompanying the search party. Constable Allwood was also included in it, and, under the leadership of Sub-Inspector Pewtress, the police and five civilians set out about six o'clock from Mansfield as the sun was going down. The party were well mounted, for the smallest bush township is never deficient in horseflesh, but they were miserably armed—two rifles, which the constables had been able to borrow, being their only weapons. The township was left, by this draft upon its resources, almost defenceless.

As far as Monk's saw-mill, distant about thirteen miles from Mansfield, and situated in comparatively settled country, no difficulty arose about the route. On arrival there a guide was necessary, and Mr. Pewtress called up Mr. Monk, told him of the murders, and asked him for direction and assistance. It was then about half-past nine. Rain was falling in torrents and the night was pitchy dark. Mr. Monk at once consented to guide the party to Stringy Bark Creek, also inducing two of his men to join it; and at ten o'clock the searchers resumed their journey, riding in melancholy silence in single file through the forest, with no sound but the rain pattering on the leaves, an occasional mournful cry of a mopoke, or the crashing of a wallaby through the undergrowth. None but bushmen born and bred could have steered a course through such country on such a night; but under Monk's leadership the creek was reached sometime after midnight, and dismounting from their horses the party began their search for the bodies. Only the police inspector, the constables and one volunteer entered upon this melancholy work, the other men waiting with the horses about a quarter of mile from the camp. The bodies of Lonigan and Scanlon were soon discovered where they had fallen in the comparatively open ground. Striking matches to examine them, the police were able to see that they had both been shot in several places, and that they lay upon their backs; while their pockets, which were turned inside out, had been rifled of everything they contained. No signs were seen of Kennedy, and recognising that further search by night was useless, the police sat down upon a log—the same log from which McIntyre had seen his comrades approaching a few hours before—and waited for daylight. Then the other men came up and inspected the dead bodies and the camp, before making search for Kennedy.

Ashes where the tent had stood showed that it had been burnt down, and all the property possessed by the police had been either removed or destroyed by the bushrangers. The horses, which, next to the firearms, were the prize most coveted by the Kellys, were, of course, nowhere to be seen.

For a long time, with heavy rain falling, the search party diligently beat through the scrub and grass-trees searching for Kennedy, whom they had little hope of finding alive, but neither were they able to discover his body, and at last Sub-Inspector Pewtress gave orders for a start upon the journey home. Dr. Reynolds had examined the bodies of the murdered men and assured himself that by no possibility could any life be left in them, so nothing remained but to convey them back to Mansfield for inquest and burial. How to carry them was a question which presented some difficulty; but the police inspector, who had puzzled the men at the saw-mill by asking for a rope, had foreseen the task in hand. The bodies were roped together, and slung like packs, one on either side a horse's back. The horse chosen to carry this burden seemed to have some instinctive horror of travelling with it. The weight did not trouble him; but, looking backward, he could see his ghastly load; and eventually he was only persuaded to stir from the spot where he stood when blindfolded by Mr. Pewtress.

To Monk's saw-mill the journey was a gruesome one. Part of it lay through thickets of dead wattles, brittle sticks that snap and cut, and tear with their sharp ragged edges. In addition, therefore, to the melancholy caused by the death of the constables, those who escorted them had the horror of seeing their faces and inert limbs bruised and disfigured by the trees and bushes, against which the horse bumped them as he forced his way through the forest.

When Monk's saw-mill was reached this painful phase of the journey concluded; for a vehicle with four horses was in waiting, provided at the police officer's request by Mr Kitchen, a leading resident, who gave great assistance to the police. Thence unto Mansfield the cavalcade followed the vehicle until near the town, when some of the horsemen galloped on to tell the people what they had discovered of the murders. The bodies were conveyed to the dead-room of the hospital to await the inquest which soon followed, and Mr Pewtress was busied in dealing with a pile of telegrams and correspondence relative to the outrage, the news of which, by this time, have been flashed everywhere and created a profound sensation throughout Australia. Three or four constables, from different outlaying districts, had arrived, under orders from headquarters, at When dusk came on the members of the party, in spite of Sub-Inspector Pewtress' remonstrances, positively refused to remain for the night upon the ground, but insisted upon returning to Mansfield. panic, were not satisfied with the arrangements made for their defence.

Mrs. Kennedy, wife of the missing Sergeant Kennedy, who resided in Mansfield, was the object of universal sympathy and commiseration. The uncertainty as to her husband's fate was terribly hard to bear, and few people dared hold out hope to her of ever seeing him again alive. McIntyre was unable to say anything as to the seriousness of his wound, but he was a good officer who had been concerned before in the arrest of cattle-stealers—friends of the Kellys—and they had given proof of bloodthirstiness which left little room to hope for mercy from them to their enemies. During the day an inquest was held upon the bodies of Scanlon and Lonigan, in both of which numerous bullet wounds were found, some of them apparently inflicted after death. McIntyre, who gave evidence at the inquest, repeated the story which he had given to Sub-Inspector Pewtress, and nothing else to throw light upon the matter was forthcoming. Some little excitement was caused in the town by the arrest of two brothers, named "Wild" Wright and "Dummy" Wright, friends of the Kellys, who were well known to the police and supposed to be sympathisers with the bushrangers. They were charged, on this occasion, with using threatening language to members of the search party, and showed considerable resistance, when they were locked up.

In the meantime the police had been busy in organising a second search party to look for Kennedy, which started for Stringy Bark Creek on Tuesday. When the men arrived at the camp it was late in the afternoon, and during the hours of daylight remaining, the ground was searched carefully, but without success.

When dusk came on the members of the party, in spite of Sub-Inspector Pewtress' remonstrances, positively refused to remain for the night upon the ground, but insisted upon returning to Mansfield. It was useless for the police officer to remain alone, as many men were wanted for the search; so he perforce accompanied the others on their return, leaving, on his way, some of the constables at Monk's saw-mill for its protection, since it was thought the bushrangers might still be lurking in the neighbourhood.

When Sub-Inspector Pewtress returned to Mansfield, he found that other constables had arrived, and also the chief officer in charge of the district, Superintendent Sadlier.

By this time Mr. Pewtress was almost worn out by his continued exertion and responsibility, while McIntyre had broken down, and was ill in the hospital.

Mr. Pewtress, however, accompanied the third search party—a large one, composed of police and civilians, which he and Superintendent Sadleir had collected—and set out again as soon as possible for the scene of the tragedy.

There, about eight o'clock on Thursday morning, the question of Kennedy's fate was solved at last. More than a quarter of a mile from the camp, Mr. Tompkins, President of the Shire Council, came upon a body covered with a cloak. It was Kennedy, shot through the forehead and disfigured with numerous other wounds.

Lapse of time and the attacks of insects had made his features almost unrecognisable; but there was no difficulty in identifying the body, and, like those of his unfortunate comrades, it was slung upon a horse for conveyance through the bush to the saw-mills, whence a vehicle took it on to Mansfield.

There an inquest was held; but necessarily no further evidence was forthcoming than had been available in the case of the other murders. Medical examination, however, showed that a wound in the chest had been made by a charge from a shot-gun fired at close range. The muzzle, in fact, must have been held almost against the wounded man's breast as he lay helpless, and the shot was probably fired from his own gun.

Sergeant Kennedy's funeral, which was one of the largest ever witnessed in the district, was attended by clergy of all denominations, among them Dr Moorhouse, Anglican Bishop of Melbourne, and quantities of flowers were sent to do honour to a brave man and testify the sympathy felt for his widow. The Government generously recognised her claims upon it, by deciding that the late sergeant's full pay should be given to her for the support of herself and her children. After the funeral Mansfield, gradually recovering its equilibrium, turned its attention to the chances of capturing the miscreants, and the facts connected with the outrage. Of the latter it was impossible to learn much; but it was ascertained that Kennedy had been informed of the proximity of the Kellys to the police camp. He had not communicated that fact to McIntyre, and it was surmised that his informant had treacherously told the Kellys that Kennedy was going in search of them. They, it appeared, had inhabited a hut, with mud walls, which was almost a fortress, on the site of some deserted alluvial diggings, not far from the scene of murder. Complaints were loud in Mansfield of the shockingly inadequate arming of the police who, by this time, had gone in pursuit of the bushrangers. One party of seven police had only four rifles between them; but these matters were gradually attended to, and Mansfield itself was mollified by a strong force of constables being stationed in the town, and the despatch of twenty-five rifles from Melbourne for the defence of the inhabitants.

3
THE BUSHRANGERS' COUNTRY

IT was not only in Mansfield and the district immediately connected with the crime that public feeling was excited and alarmed by the police murders, which surpassed in cold-blooded audacity any former exploits of bushranging gangs in Victoria. All over the colony nothing was talked of but the Kelly outrage. The press of Melbourne and the country towns was full of it, while there was immense activity in the police department, which despatched heavy reinforcements of constabulary to every township in the North-East.

For many years this portion of Victoria had enjoyed an unenviable notoriety as the home of cattle "duffers" and other lawless persons; and two of the most notorious bush-rangers of former years, Morgan and Power, had both been at home in the river valleys and heavily forested ranges that cover much of the country. Only ten years before Power, a solitary rover, who had terrorised a large part of the colony by his "sticking-up" exploits, though murder was a crime of which he was never guilty, had been captured on the top of a mountain some fifteen miles distant from the scene of the Kelly outrage. Morgan, a blood-thirsty villain, to whom murder was rather a pleasure than otherwise, was well know and hated by the farmers of the district before he became an outlaw. Two or three miles from the scene of Power's capture he had been wounded by a charge of shot fired at him by a squatter who chanced upon him in the bush, but had escaped capture and hidden himself away until, later, he was shot dead, while going to seek his horse at Peechelba, a station he had stuck up upon the New South Wales border.

While Power and Morgan were the men whose deeds were most flagrant in the district, cattle-stealing and other minor crimes were common there, and the police were kept constantly on the alert. The popularity of cattle "duffing" in the neighbourhood may be accounted for, partly by the fact that it was largely settled by men of bad and lawless antecedents, and partly by the tremendous temptations to criminal adventure which the conditions of the country afforded. The King, the Ovens, and the Buffalo, the Broken River, and a number of minor rivers and creeks, all flow through fertile valleys, sparsely settled by farmers and graziers, into plain country, much of which is thickly forested; and all the streams have trackless ranges not far distant from either bank. North of these is the Murray River, forming the border of New South Wales and

Victoria, and also flowing, in its upper reaches, through a jumble of hills and mountains, while the headwaters of all the rivers named are absolutely uninhabited mountain country, stretching east and north for hundreds of miles.

Even the towns of some importance on the plains are all adjacent to ranges containing innumerable hiding-places. Mansfield lies embosomed in mountains, at the terminus of a line (not then constructed) which branches away from the main North-Eastern railway many miles to the south. Wangaratta, Glenrowan, Benalla, and Euroa—stations upon the North- Eastern and Sydney line—though they are situated themselves on flat and open country, are all flanked by adjacent wooden ranges. Beechworth, the northern-most of the important Victorian towns, in what is called the "Kelly" country, forms the terminus of another branch line, and is picturesquely situated at an altitude of some thousands of feet in the heart of the mountains. A careful study of the map of Victoria and of the relative positions of the towns and rivers named would be necessary to enable anyone to follow the doings of the outlaws and the police with proper understanding of the exploits of the former, and the terrible difficulties of the latter in attempting to capture them.

Enough has probably been said, however, to explain the temptations and opportunities which the country offered to cattle and horse stealers, who were encouraged in their pursuits by the conduct of law-abiding, honest stock-owners almost as much as by Nature. While comparatively very little of the country was fenced, cattle and horses belonging to different individuals were allowed to run together far from the homesteads, in the good land by the banks of creeks and rivers in the mountains, where their owners, who were, almost without exception, splendid bushmen, could periodically inspect them, and muster them when required. This casual system of grazing would have worked better than it did but for the fact that dishonest adventurers, who were also skilled bushmen, found it easy to muster other people's stock. Having done so, they drove them away by devious mountain tracks to some distant market, generally in New South Wales, and disposed of them, often months before their owners knew that they had suffered loss. A favourite plan was to impound Victorian horses or cattle in the pounds of New South Wales border towns, purchase them for the trifle which impounded stock usually bring, and then resell them to innocent buyers, to whom the thieves were able to give an apparently good title. The police of New South Wales and Victoria, who were both well aware of the plan of operation, were in constant communication with one another, and effected many captures of adventurous horse and cattle stealers. Until the whole of the professional "duffing" population was either safely under lock and key in the gaols, or, at least, had experienced a term there, and so lost caste with their admirers, who worshipped, and were only too ready to emulate unpunished "smartness", the police felt that it would be futile to hope for a full measure of law and order in the district. The Kellys themselves were well known cattle thieves, with whom the police had considerable acquaintance. Mr. Nicholson, the Victorian Inspecting Police Superintendent, on a visit to the North-East two years before the murders, had reported specially upon the Kelly family, and had advised the removal of a police constable from the neighbourhood of Greta, a small township near which the Kellys lived, on the ground that a man of superior attainments was needed for such a responsible post. Portion of his report, dated April, 1877, is worth quoting. The Kellys' house, it may be said, is about four miles distant from Greta, on the road to Benalla.

Mr. Nicholson writes as follows:—"I visited the notorious Mrs. Kelly's house on the road from hence to Benalla. She lived on a piece of cleared and partly cultivated land on the road-side, in an old wooden hut, with a large bark roof. The dwelling was divided into five apartments by partitions of blanketing, rugs, &c. There were no men in the house, only women and two girls of about fourteen years of age, said to be her daughters. They all appeared to be existing in poverty and squalor. She said her sons were out at work, but did not indicate where, and that their relatives seldom came near them. However, their communications with each other are known to the police. Until the gang referred to is rooted out of this neighbourhood, one of the most experienced and successful mounted constables in the district will be required in charge of Greta. I do not think the present arrangements are sufficient. Second-class Sergeant Steele, of Wangaratta, keeps the offenders referred to under as good surveillance as the distance and means at his command will permit. But I submit that Constable Thorn would hardly be able to cope with these men. At the same time some of these offenders may commit themselves foolishly someday, and may be apprehended and convicted in a very ordinary manner."

This report is important, as showing the class of men with whom the police had to deal, and the fact that responsible officers well recognised the gravity of the position, long before it culminated so tragically.

The Kellys belonged to a very numerous clan, most of whose member had been more or less in bad odour with the police. John Kelly, the father of the bushrangers, and a native of Ireland, had begun his troubles in the old country, whence he was transported for fifteen years to Tasmania—on his own account for no worse offence than being concerned in a faction fight at a fair. From Tasmania, on his release, he emigrated to Victoria, and, after following various occupations, mining among them, he settled on the Eleven-mile Creek, near Greta, where his family continued to reside after his death. In Victoria he received, at one time, a sentence of six months' imprisonment for being in possession of beef, presumably the carcass of a stolen bullock; but he appears, on the whole, to have led a fairly peaceful and harmless life. His wife, and the mother of the bushrangers, belonged to a large family of Quinns, many of whom had a bad record. It was near their house on the Glenmore run, on the upper reaches of the King River, that the bushranger Power was captured by Superintendents Nicholson and Hare in 1870, and it was well known that the Quinns were in league with Power, and always gave him warning of the approach of the police to his haunts. Mr. Hare relates that, besides numerous dogs of various breeds which barked loudly on strangers' approach, and could be heard by Power in his hut or "gunyah" on the mountain nearby, the Quinns kept a peacock, whose scream was also a danger signal to the outlaw. It was only because the police, who were forced, by trackless scrub and flood-swollen creeks, to pass close by the Quinns' house, did so on a night of storm and rain that the sentries, which had taken shelter from the elements, failed to warn Power when the search-party was creeping up the mountain to arrest him.

Ned Kelly, in his boyhood, spent much time with his relatives at Glenmore, and appears to have been on intimate terms with Power, though he was associated in none of his robberies, never getting further than helping him to reconnoitre the country, or taking charge of Power's horses at a distance. At this time Kelly was a boy of about sixteen, of whose courage or daring Power thought very little, while he, on his part, was afraid of Power's ungovernable temper, and always ready to leave him at a moment's notice.

The remainder of the Kelly family at the time when serious trouble began, consisted of the old lady, née Quinn. Dan — the second outlaw — Jim, and four sisters — Mrs. Gunn, Mrs. Skillion, Kate, and Grace. Ned, the eldest of the family, was born 1854; Dan in 1861, but though so much younger than his brother, he had been mixed up with several of the former's horse and cattle stealing exploits, and had an unenviable reputation as being a vicious, cunning little sneak, in addition to a law-breaker. James Kelly, Ned's other brother, who took no part in their more serious crimes, was arrested with Dan, when the latter was only ten years old, for illegally using horses — a step in the apprenticeship to regular stealing; but both boys were discharged on account of their youth. Later on, in conjunction with a man named Williamson, he received four years imprisonment for cattle stealing. Other members of what were known to the police as the "Kelly mob", were John Lloyd, married to the sister of Mrs. Quinn, and his sons, Tom and Paddy Lloyd, who lived near their relatives, the Kellys, and were also continually in collision with the police, Lloyd senior, some years before the Kelly outbreak, being imprisoned for four years for maliciously killing a neighbour's horse. Steve Hart, a third member of the gang who murdered the constables, and Joe Byrne, the fourth, had also both been known as cattle or horse-stealers, but enjoyed by no means so evil a notoriety as the Kellys. At the time of the murder in the Wombat Ranges, near Mansfield, it was not known that they were the Kellys' partners in the outrage, and for some time afterwards suspicion rested on other men.

Hart, who was only eighteen years old, was born near Wangaratta, and there his family resided close by the Warby Ranges, with the intricacies of which Hart was well acquainted.

Joe Byrne, three years older that Hart, a fine, handsome young man, apparently with many good qualities, had been at school in Beechworth, near which, at a place called Woolshed he resided, and he was as much at home in the mountains of his locality as were the Kellys with the interminable ranges behind Greta, and Hart with the Warby Ranges. The fact that between them the bushrangers were so intimately acquainted with an immense tract of country, covering thousands of square miles, with sympathisers and hiding-places in every part of it, was one of the factors which enabled them so long to baffle the police.

Another factor was the frequent removal of constables from their stations just as they were beginning to win the confidence of the people and know the district. But for the injudicious removal from Greta of Senior-Constable Flood, who had prosecuted at one time or another the whole of the Kelly mob, and who could find his way through the bush almost as well as the Kellys themselves, the Kelly murders might never have been committed, for Flood was feared as well as hated by the lawbreakers, and during his term at Greta he had some of the Kelly family nearly always in gaol. At any rate, if he, and more men such as he, had been in the Kelly district when the murders did take place, the career of the outlaws would probably have been much shorter than it eventually proved to be.

4
WHY THE KELLYS "WENT OUT"

ON the 15th of April, 1878, six months prior to the Wombat murders, Constable Fitzpatrick, then stationed at Benalla, the headquarters of the North-Eastern District Police, saddled his horse and rode quietly over to Greta, a distance of about fifteen miles. He was bound on a visit to the Kellys, since he had read in the "Police Gazette" that Dan Kelly and John Lloyd, the members of the family who happened to be in trouble at the time, were wanted on a charge of horse-stealing. The warrant was not in his possession, but that circumstance was of no consequence, and he hoped, perchance, to find Dan Kelly at home. The sergeant approved of Fitzpatrick's expedition, but told him to be careful, as the Kellys were known to be dangerous characters, quite likely to resist an arrest, to which Fitzpatrick replied that he knew what he was doing, and everything would be right.

When he arrived at the Kelly residence, which was a new hut built at some distance from the old one, no one was at home except Mrs Kelly and some of the younger children. With them Fitzpatrick spent a few minutes talking, but did not mention the object of his visit, to which, though Mrs Kelly might have guessed it, since warrants were out against both her sons, she also made no reference.

Fitzpatrick was on better terms with the Kelly family than constables were wont to be, for on one occasion, when he had arrested Ned Kelly for drunkenness, he did not press the charge, and this was accounted to him for righteousness. Accordingly, perhaps also being aware that a warrant for Dan's arrest had yet been issued, Mrs. Kelly remained talking to Fitzpatrick, till he, hearing the sound of someone cutting wood on a creek near the hut, rode away through the timber to see who the splitter might be, and whether he had a splitter's license. The man, one Williamson, who lived with the Kellys, and who was splitting fence rails, explained that he needed no license, since he was not working on Crown lands, and Fitzpatrick, with apparently no police duty on hand, was riding away towards Greta when he saw two horsemen passing through a slip panel towards the Kellys' old hut. He rode in their direction, and when he reached them, found Skillion, one of Mrs Kelly's sons-in-law, with his own horse, leading the other from which the saddle and bridle had been taken, while the rider had disappeared. Asked to whom the unsaddled horse belonged, Skillion said he did not know, which, as the rider had been Skillion's companion, Fitzpatrick naturally did not believe, and studying the horse attentively, he recognized it. "Why, that is Dan Kelly's mare," he said.

Skillion admitted it, and when the constable asked where he had gone, supposed that he was up at the house, that is, the new hut. Accordingly Fitzpatrick rode back, and called to Dan, who, with his hat and coat off, and with a knife and fork in his hand, came out of the door.

"Dan", said Fitzpatrick, "I am going to arrest you on a charge of horse-stealing."

"All right," was the answer, "but I've been riding all day, and I'm having something to eat. I suppose you will wait till then?"

Fitzpatrick said he would, and, tying up his horse, went in to join the party, where he was welcomed with abuse by Mrs Kelly, who said he was "a deceitful little — — —," and that he should not take Dan out of the house that night. Dan, according to Fitzpatrick, was much more reasonable, and went on with his meal, so far agreeing with the constable as to say, "Shut up, mother; that's all right," when she objected to Fitzpatrick's assurance that there was no need to quarrel, merely because he had to do his duty.

Fitzpatrick had scarcely been three minutes in the house, when Ned Kelly entered suddenly, and exclaiming, "Out of this you — — —," fired a shot at Fitzpatrick from his revolver. It did not hit him, but Mrs. Kelly rushed in to the fight, and struck Fitzpatrick on the head with a fire shovel, smashing his helmet down over his eyes. As Fitzpatrick raised his arm to defend himself, Ned Kelly fired a second shot, which struck him in the wrist, and when he turned to draw his revolver, he discovered that Dan Kelly had taken it while his attention was engaged, and was now covering him with it. By this time Williamson, the rail-splitter, had also arrived upon the scene, entering the kitchen from an adjoining bed-room, and he too had a revolver, while immediately afterwards came Skillion with another, which he pointed at Fitzpatrick.

Any arrest was clearly out of the question for a time, and as Ned Kelly grasped Fitzpatrick's arm, the latter fell to the ground, and Kelly, he says, recognising him for the first time, exclaimed, "That will do, boys; if I had known it was Fitzpatrick, I wouldn't have fired a bloody shot."

After this Fitzpatrick became, for a short time, unconscious, and when he came to himself and rose, Ned Kelly insisted upon taking out the bullet, which was a very small one, and not deeply imbedded in the constable's wrist. Ned was anxious to use a razor for the purpose, to which Fitzpatrick, not liking amateur surgery, objected, begging to be allowed to go to a doctor in Benalla, but Kelly was insistent, and finally consented to prise out the bullet with the penknife which Fitzpatrick took out of his own pocket.

It was about dusk when this occurred, but the Kellys and their friends would not let Fitzpatrick depart, keeping him in the hut till eleven o'clock, when he mounted his horse and rode away through Winton to Benalla, and reported his misadventure.

The above is Fitzpatrick's version of the affair, upon which the police and the Criminal Court acted, for Mrs Kelly, Williamson, and Skillion, who were all arrested, received very heavy sentences for their alleged assault upon Fitzpatrick. The constable's version was, however, afterwards corroborated by Williamson, who, during the course of his six years' imprisonment, was interviewed in Pentridge by the Chief Commissioner of Police, Captain Standish, and backed up every word of Fitzpatrick's evidence. It was, on the other hand, absolutely denied in all essentials by Skillion, Mrs Kelly, and Ned Kelly, who swore that he was hundreds of miles away on the occasion, and stated that Skillion was not present either. Ned's version of the matter, based on information from Dan, is that Mrs. Kelly advised him not to go unless the constable could produce a warrant, and that Fitzpatrick thereupon drew his revolver, threatening to blow Mrs Kelly's brains out if she interfered, to which the old lady replied that he would be less free with his pop-gun were Ned anywhere about. Dan cunningly called out, "Here is Ned coming now," and as Fitzpatrick, taken in by the ruse, turned his head, Dan snatched the revolver from him, emptied it, returned it, and allowed Fitzpatrick to go away unharmed. Fitzpatrick's wound, which was very slight, Dan declares was self-inflicted.

The fact that Fitzpatrick had been drinking, or at least had taken more than one glass on his way to the Kellys' that day, and was afterwards dismissed from the force, on the ground that he associated with the lowest people in the township, could not be trusted out of sight, and never did his duty, naturally inclined many people to doubt the strict accuracy of his story. A popular theory was that he had behaved in a blackguard way towards the Kellys' unmarried sister, Kate, and thus incurred the enmity of her brothers, but to this Ned himself gave the most emphatic denial, and, as Captain Standish stated, one of the prisoners, Williamson afterwards said that Fitzpatrick spoke the truth about the encounter. The constable's story is therefore the most reliable of those extant, and upon its acceptance, as fact hinged the after events that make the Kelly gang's history. Mrs Kelly, Skillion, and Williamson went to gaol, and Ned and Dan Kelly, for whose arrest the Government offered a reward of £200, disappeared from sight, and were never seen by the police again until they encountered and shot Kennedy and his party on the banks of the creek in the Wombat Ranges.

Dan Kelly and Constable Fitzpatrick.—

5
POLICE PREPARATIONS

AT the time the murders were committed the police of Victoria were under the command of Captain Standish, a retired military officer, who held the position of Chief Commissioner, while the officers under him who played leading parts in the events which followed were Mr Charles Hope Nicolson, Assistant Commissioner; Superintendent Sadleir and Superintendent Hare, all of the Victorian police force; and Mr. Stanhope O'Connor, a Queensland officer, whose services were borrowed by Victoria at a later date, together with those of a party of black trackers under his command. Mr. Sadleir, with his headquarters at Benalla, was in charge of the North-Eastern police district, which comprised an area of nearly 11,000 square miles, much of it mountainous and uninhabited country; while the total number of police charged with the duty of keeping order therein did not exceed 120.

On the news of the murders reaching Melbourne Captain Standish promptly sent reinforcements, not only to Mansfield, but to Beechworth, Benalla, Wangaratta, and many other stations in the disturbed district, and on the main line of railway from Melbourne to Sydney. At the same time, after communication with the Chief Secretary, he dispatched Spencer rifles and such other arms as the Department had in stock, and obtained authority for the purchase of a number of double-barrelled breech- loading guns. In these measures he was influenced, not only by the desire to capture the Kellys and to protect peaceful citizens from their raids, but by a deep distrust of many of the inhabitants of the Kelly district, who were known to be sympathisers with the outlaws. In giving evidence before a Royal Commission on the Police Force of Victoria in 1881, Captain Standish mentioned some facts serving to make more intelligible the apparently great strain which the pursuit of four miscreants put upon the resources of the colony. "The Kellys, as is well known," he said, "had an enormous number of sympathisers in the district, and after their outrages there is not the slightest doubt that a great many respectable men were in dread of their lives, and were intimidated by a fear of the consequences from giving any information whatsoever to the police. Not only the lives of those of their families were in danger, but their sheep and horses and cattle and property were liable to be stolen or destroyed; in addition to which there is not the slightest doubt that there was an enormous number of tradesmen in the district who were so benefitted by the large increase of police, and the consequent expenditure, that they were only too glad that this unpleasant business was protracted for so many months.

"I may also state that a great many of the local papers never lost an opportunity of attacking the police in the most unjustifiable manner, and on every possible occasion; and remarks of that kind, as I think every sensible man must be aware, were not only calculated to do the police a great deal of harm, but to prevent their receiving material assistance from anybody."

In these remarks Captain Standish by no means exaggerated the difficulty of the position from the police point of view, while it was alleged by many civilians that some members of the police, who received extra pay while on Kelly-hunting duty, were not too anxious to capture their game and and go back to the inactive barracks scale of pay. Most of them, however, undoubtedly did their duty with the utmost zeal, even in cases where experience and intelligence were wanting, and the nature of the district and the people imposed a most formidable task upon the police in pursuit of the bushrangers.

In addition to the despatch of constables and arms, Captain Standish's first active move was the sending of Superintendent Nicolson to Benalla to take command of Kelly operations, leaving Superintendent Sadlier in ordinary charge of his district, with the understanding that he also was to assist in every way in his power with the most important work in hand. Accordingly, on October 28—the same day on which news of the murders reached Melbourne—Superintendent Nicolson left the city by the Sydney train for Benalla, and, arriving there that evening, found the township in a great state of excitement. Two other small police parties in addition to Kennedy's were at that time absent from their stations in search of the Kellys, and considerable anxiety was felt lest they should have suffered the same fate; but in the course of a day or two they returned safe.

When Superintendent Nicolson arrived Superintendent Sadlier was absent from Benalla in another part of the district. He returned on the morning of October 29, and rode over to Mansfield, where he gave instructions to Sub-Inspector Pewtress regarding the search for the body of Kennedy, and then returned to duty at Benalla. At Mans-field Mr. Sadlier found in the lock-up Isaiah Wright, commonly known as "Wild" Wright, a noted Kelly sympathiser frequently in collision with the police, whose name indicates well enough his reputation; and the police officer promised him £30 if he would go and find the body of Kennedy, or bring him into Mansfield, if alive. "Wild" Wright started on his mission, his intention being to see Mrs. Skillion, Ned's sister, and learn from her

Kennedy's whereabouts; but before he could do anything in the matter, the body was found, under circumstances already described. . This arrangement with "Wild" Wright was the first instance, after the Kelly murders, of the employment of private "agents" by the police—a system which afterwards attained to considerable dimensions and importance. Previous to this, Detective Ward, a Victorian officer, had been travelling through the district unknown to the ordinary police, making inquiries as to the Kellys' whereabouts, and it was owing to information supplied by him that the search parties, including Kennedy's which so disastrously encountered the outlaws, were put upon their tracks. Superintendent Sadlier, however, wishing for more accurate knowledge, had proposed to Captain Standish to employ an agent to supplement Ward's endeavours, and on August 29 wrote as follows:—

"Dear Captain Standish,—I am a good deal exercised in mind at hearing, as often as I do, of Ned Kelly being about. He is not likely to fall into our hands by ordinary means, and I think of proposing to a young acquaintance of mine, of the criminal class, to spend a few weeks in the places where he is supposed to haunt, and endeavour to lay us on to him. I am sure, if this trap were known to Kelly or his associates, the young fellow's life would not be worth much. They would not be any the wiser, unless the young fellow himself talks about it. It would require a few pounds to give the young fellow a start. I can only say he is bad enough, I believe, to do anything in the prospect of the reward. I should be glad to learn from you if you would like the proposition. By letter posted on Saturday, or a telegram till Monday, will find me at Mansfield, where my protege lives."

Captain Standish did like the proposition, but his answer arrived too late for Mr. Sadlier to act upon it, and the incident is only mentioned here as a further indication of the strange sources of information to which the authorities were driven, and the very undesirable proteges whom, to further the ends of justice, they were oblige to take under their wing. Without being able to take any further steps Mr. Sadlier returned to Benalla, and during the next few days there appeared in the Mansfield papers circumstantial and elaborate accounts of the way in which Kennedy met his death. These accounts doubtless filtered through from members of the Kelly family, and were contributed to the press by friends or sympathisers, under a pledge of secrecy as to the informants which was scrupulously preserved. The Kelly account of Kennedy's shooting differed considerably from that of McIntyre in so far that the sergeant was reported to have kept up a brisk fire on the outlaws before he fell wounded by them, but Ned Kelly admitted that he gave Kennedy his coup de grace while lying on the ground. It was from merciful motives, he said, since he could not find it in his heart to leave a wounded man alone in the bush; but other reports said that Kennedy had begged hard for a chance to live as long as he could, that perchance he might see his wife and children again before he died. At any rate, the statements of eye witnesses bore out the conclusion at which the medical had arrived by examination of the body—namely, that the gun-shot wound had been inflicted by a charge fired from a muzzle held almost against the unfortunate man's breast.

There were other mysteries in connection with the affair which have never been wholly cleared up, and it appears now, not only that many of the people near Mansfield had exact knowledge of the Kellys' position in a fortified hut near Stringy Bark Creek, but that from some private source of information Kennedy knew far more about the matter than McIntyre or Lonigan. Also it seems that there must have been an eye-witness of the tragedy unknown to McIntyre, who saw only the four outlaws. Such, at any rate, seems the only explanation of the fact that a mysterious traveller, who was never identified, riding through Strathbogie on Sunday evening, when McIntyre was wearily making his way towards Mansfield, told people whom he met: "There are two or three police shot in the country." He indicated the direction of the Wombat Ranges with his hand, and said no more, and his statement was put down as an idle tale until McIntyre's report confirmed it. Sunday evening is the time now accepted as that when this report reached the ears of people at Strathbogie, twenty miles from the scene of the murders. But Saturday, the day of the tragedy, was the date given to an agent of Mr Sadlier's by very respectable men who claimed to have heard it. Mr Sadlier considers that they mistook the day—the truth of their statements he did not doubt. This may be so; but, on the other hand, the informant may have ridden away at top speed; while another possible and somehow gruesome explanation of the mystery is that the Kellys, who doubtless were perfectly acquainted with the movements of the police, had deliberately planned to surround the camp by Stringy Bark Creek, and murder its occupants.

In such a case the rumour on Saturday may have been a prediction of events from one who had been in the Kellys' confidence, and had left their society before they stained their hands with murder.

On the evening after the Kellys had completed their work they had a visitor in the person of one of the Lloyds, belonging to the family of friends and sympathisers already mentioned. He, however, could not have been responsible for the report received at Strathbogie, for, according to information afterwards received, his part in the matter was confined to keeping guard outside the Kellys' stronghold while they slept for a few hours to refresh themselves, after which they saddled up the police horses and rode away through the ranges to their friends at Greta, some thirty miles from Stringy Bark Creek.

Victorian police recreate events at Stringy Bark Creek.

6
MR. NICOLSON IN PURSUIT. – THE OUTLAWRY BILL.

WHILE Mr. Sadlier was absent at Mansfield Mr. Nicolson had not been idle. From Benalla, Wangaratta, and Beechworth parties were immediately sent out in pursuit of the outlaws, but even then it was recognised that in such an extent of country the quest resembled searching for a needle in a bundle of hay. Mr. Nicolson himself did not remain at Benalla, but went on to personally superintend matters at Wangaratta, and afterwards at Myrtleford, a pretty mountain township, now a great tourist resort in the north- eastern portion of the district. Rumours of the Kellys' appearance came thick and fast in bewildering numbers, and from places so far apart — in many cases hundreds of miles — that in spite of the bushrangers' marvellous celerity of movement it was clear that most of them must be false. However, on November 1 it was rumoured that a selector had been stuck up by the gang near the residence of a man named Baumgarten, on the Murray Flats. Baumgarten had been convicted of horse-stealing, and was a known associate of the bushrangers, who had often visited his house, besides which it was exceedingly probable that they would make a break away from the district, and try to conceal themselves for a time in the rough country in New South Wales beyond the Murray River. Accordingly Mr. Nicolson and Mr. Sadlier, after consulting together, decided that this particular rumour was worth careful investigation and action thereon, with the result that a police party was immediately dispatched to Wodonga, the border town on the Victorian side of the Murray, connected by a bridge with the New South Wales town of Albury on the other side. No news arrived from this party, which was under the direction of Detective Kennedy, and Mr. Nicolson himself therefore took the train for Wodonga, where he arrived on November 2 and interviewed his men. They told him that Margery, the farmer who alleged he had been stuck up, was off his head with drink, and that they placed no credence in his story; but Mr. Nicolson, still unsatisfied, interviewed Margery himself. He had certainly been drinking, as Mr. Nicolson thought, to drown his fright, but he was then sober again, and gave a clear and connected account of his experiences, describing the outlaws in such a manner as to convince Mr Nicolson that he had seen them. Mrs Baumgarten also, whose house lay about a mile and a half from the river, said she had seen the men come out of some lagoons near the Murray close to her house and camp till sunset some 200 yards away. Mr Nicolson found the camp, but the birds had frown. The police officer had with him an aboriginal from the River Darling, who was an intelligent tracker, and from the camp he followed the man's tracks southward for some distance, but lost them when darkness came on. Thus nothing came of the information, but afterwards, for the news was never difficult to obtain when it was useless, the police learned that they had been very close upon their men. They ascertained too, with considerable exactitude, what the outlaws' movements had been after the murder of the police on October 26.

On the Saturday evening, with young Lloyd standing sentry by their hut, they had spent a few hours in sleep, and had made a start in the small hours of Sunday morning across uninhabited country, to Greta. There they spent most of the day, no doubt, discussing future plans with their relatives and friends. On Monday evening on horseback they passed through the townships of Oxley and Everton, making north for New South Wales; and at a public house, known as Moon's Pioneer Hotel, on the Ovens River, some twenty miles from Greta, they had purchased grog, some tins of sardines and other provisions. On October 30 they were seen by the farmer Margery near the banks of the Murray, nearly thirty miles from Everton, and they appear to have made strenuous attempts to cross the river into New South Wales. At Bungowunnah wharf, on the Victorian side, they found a punt, of which they had hoped to avail themselves, sunk in the stream, and there was no possibility of swimming the river. The Murray, which is at times the mere brown thread, is liable to floods, and when they come the low lying banks on either side become one vast lagoon, with islands peeping out here and there. The men appear to had ventured deep into the lagoons in the hope of reaching the main stream, but were forced to abandon the attempt, for the river was higher than it had been for many years, and accordingly they turned their horses' heads southward towards their native haunts.

On November 3 they were seen in the neighbourhood of the Murray, and on the same day near Wangaratta, a township more than forty miles distant. They passed through Wangaratta during the night, and were seen next day crossing under the railway line at a place known as the One Mile Bridge, after which they disappeared in the Warby Ranges, low densely wooded mountains close to Wangaratta, with which the Kellys and Hart were all well acquainted.

This occasion seems to have offered an excellent chance of capturing the Kellys, for Sergeant Steele to whom the information was brought, with a description of the tracks, was convinced that they were actually made by the Kellys, partly from the fact that the One Mile Creek was running bank high beneath the railway bridge, and that no-one without initimate knowledge of the place could possibly have piloted the way along a narrow ledge of ground beneath, while that ledge he knew was known to Steve Hart. After the heavy rain the tracks were easy to follow. The bushrangers' horses must have been almost done after their hard riding since the previous Saturday, and Sergeant Steele considered that by an active pursuit the men might have been captured in the Warby Ranges. Nothing, however, was done. Mr Brooke Smith who was in charge of a large party of police at Wangaratta took no action, and Sergeant Steele was under orders to proceed to a place called Rats' Castle, in the granite hills near Beechworth, where the bushrangers had friends and were likely to make their appearance.

For letting this chance go by Sergeant Steele was severely blamed, as it seems most unjustly, by the Royal Commission which enquired in the matters connected with the Kelly Outbreak. On his way from Benalla to Beechworth he stopped at Wangaratta to enquire into the report of the Kellys' appearance, acting according to Mr Sadlier's instructions which were to the following effect: "You can halt the train for a time at Wangaratta while you make enquiries, and if you think there is anything in it, send word to Inspector Brooke Smith, who is in charge of a party at Wangaratta, to follow up their tracks." Accordingly Sergeant Steele sent word by Constable Twomey to Mr Brooke Smith that by Superintendent Sadlier's orders he, Mr Brooke Smith, was to start in pursuit of the bushrangers at daylight the following day. Sergeant Steele proceeded on his journey to Beechworth, and no pursuit being made by Mr Smith, Sergeant Steele was severely censured and recommended for reduction on the ranks by the Commission, a procedure which aroused the utmost indignation in Wangaratta, where Sergeant Steele's sterling services as a police officer were fully appreciated.

Up to this time, though the two Kellys were known as members of the gang of murderers, there was doubt as to the identity of the other two, and they were erroneously supposed to be identical with a certain William King of Greta, and Charles Brown, of King River, who answered somewhat to the description given by McIntyre of his assailants. Within a few days of the murders the Victorian Government passed through all its stages an Outlawry Bill under the terms of which an outlaw might be taken by any person dead or alive, provided he failed to surrender and stand his trial after due notice by proclamation. By the same Act it was provided that anyone aiding such outlaw, or withholding information about him from the police, should be liable to fifteen years' imprisonment—a provision which, if it had been strictly acted upon without a very liberal exception list, would have filled the gaols for many years with sympathetic or terrorised inhabitants of the North-Eastern District.

Under this Act on November 4, the Chief Justice, on application from the Solicitor-General, issued his warrant and granted an order calling upon the gang severally to surrender on or before November 12, to take their trial for murder. Thereupon the necessary notices and proclamations were published in the "Government Gazette" and various other papers of Melbourne and the North Eastern District, of which proclamations the following may be interesting as an example:—

To a MAN whose name is unknown, but whose person is described as follows: Nineteen or twenty years of age, five feet eight inches high, rather stout, complexion somewhat fair, no beard or whiskers, a few straggling hairs over face, rather hooked nose, sinister expression, supposed to be identical with William King, of Greta, in the said colony.

Whereas on the fourth day of November, one thousand eight hundred and seventy-eight, a bench warrant was issued in pursuance of the FELONS APPREHENSION ACT, 1878, under my hand and seal, in order to your answering and taking your trial for that on the twenty-sixth day of October, 1878, at Stringy Bark Creek, near Mansfield, in the Northern Bailiwick of the said colony, you did in company with one Edward Kelly and one Daniel Kelly and another man whose name is unknown feloniously and of malice aforethought kill and murder one Michael Scanlon.

And whereas in pursuance of THE FELONS AND APPREHENSION ACT, 1878, I did on the fourth day of November, 1878, order a summons to be inserted in the "Government Gazette" requiring you, the said man whose name is unknown, but whose person is described as aforesaid, to surrender yourself on or before the twelfth day of November, 1878, at Mansfield in the said colony of Victoria, to abide your trial for the before-mentioned crime, of which you the said man, whose name is unknown, but whose person is described as foresaid, stand accused.

These are therefore to will and require you, the said man whose name is unknown, but whose person is described as foresaid, to surrender yourself on or before the twelfth day of November, 1878, at Mansfield, in the said colony of Victoria, to abide your trial for the above-mentioned crime of which you stand accused, and hereof you are not to fail at your peril.

Given under my hand an seal, at Melbourne, this fourth day of November, in the year of our Lord, 1878,

WILLIAM F. STAWELL,

Chief Justice of the Supreme Court of the Colony of Victoria.

The other notices are identical with the above, except that those to Edward and Daniel Kelly are addressed to them by name, while the third notice is addressed "To a man whose name is unknown, but whose person is described as follows: Twenty-one years of age, five feet nine inches high, very fair beard, long on chin, fair complexion hair and moustache, supposed to be identical with Charles Brown, of King River, in the said colony."

To give the bushrangers every facility of surrendering in accordance with this proclamation, the Court House at Mansfield was kept open all day on Tuesday, November 12, but none of the gang put in an appearance. Thereupon followed a proclamation of outlawry against each of the gang individually, and a notice published in the "Government Gazette" and elsewhere, to the following effect:—

THE FELONS APPREHENSION ACT, 1878.

The particular attention of all persons in the colony is directed to the proclamations bearing even date herewith, and to the above-mentioned Act, and especially to the penalties to which Daniel Kelly, Edward Kelly, and two men whose names are unknown, but who are supposed to be identical with William King, of Greta, and Charles Brown, of King River, and all persons harbouring or assisting them, or any of them, are liable under the provisions of such Act, which are as follows:—

Section 3. If after proclamation by the Governor with the advice of the Executive Council of the fact of such adjudication shall have been published in the "Government Gazette" and in one or more Melbourne and one or more country newspapers such outlaw shall afterwards be found at large armed or there being reasonable ground to believe that he is armed it shall be lawful for any of Her Majesty's subjects whether a constable or not and without being accountable for the using of any deadly weapon in aid of such apprehension whether its use be preceded by a demand of surrender or not to apprehend or take such outlaw alive or dead.

Section 5. If after such proclamation any person shall voluntarily and knowingly harbour conceal or receive or give any aid shelter or sustenance to such outlaw or provide him with firearms or any other weapon or with ammunition or any horse equipment or other assistance or directly or indirectly give or cause to be given to him or any of his accomplices information tending or with intent to facilitate the commission by him of further crime or to enable him to escape from justice or shall withhold information or give false information concerning such outlaw from or to any officer of police or constable in quest of such outlaw the person so offending shall be liable to imprisonment with or without hard labour for such period, not exceeding fifteen years as the court shall determine and no allegation or proof by the party so offending that he was at the time under compulsion shall be deemed a defence unless he shall as soon as possible afterwards have gone before a justice of the peace or some officer of the police and then to the best of his ability given full information respecting such outlaw and made a declaration on oath voluntarily and fully of the facts connected with such compulsion.

Section 7. Any justice of the peace or officer of the police having reasonable cause to suspect that an outlaw or accused person summoned under the provisions of this Act is concealed or harboured in or on any dwelling-house or premises may alone or accompanied by any persons acting in his aid, and either by day or by night demand admission into and if refused admission may break and enter such dwelling-house or premises and therein apprehend any person whom he shall have reasonable ground for believing to be such outlaw or accused person, and may thereupon seize all arms found in or on such house or premises, and also apprehend all persons found in or about the same whom such justice or officer shall have reasonable ground for believing to have concealed harboured or otherwise succoured or assisted such outlaw or accused person. And all persons and arms so apprehended and seized shall be forthwith taken before some convenient justice of the peace to be further dealt with and disposed of according to law.

BRYAN O'LOGHLEN,
Attorney-General.
Crown Law Offices, Melbourne, November 15, 1878.

Prior to the proclamation of outlawry a reward of £500 per head was offered by the Government for the capture of the bushrangers to make police and civilians as active as possible in the pursuit.

7
THE RATS' CASTLE FIASCO

ON November 6 Captain Standish went up from Melbourne to Benalla to talk over the plan of campaign with Mr. Nicolson, who had just returned from his fruitless expedition to Wodonga, and on the same day there arrived an urgent message from Mr Sadlier at Beechworth: "Very positive information that the Kellys are concealed in a range near here. My informant is not quite sober and has been talking rather openly, but I am convinced his information is genuine; but it may be too late a day or two. I have but two constables here and the place is most difficult to approach. I have endeavoured to communicate with Steele's party of thirteen men, six of which I can be sure of coming, but I think you should send all you can by special to reach here before day; mounted and of course armed, and bring tracker. Reply."

Mr. Sadlier had just returned from a ride to some out-lying places in the hills to give instructions to parties of police, and on his arrival in Beechworth at half-past ten at night found the place as he says, "over run with armed men"—not police for the most part, but enthusiastic civilians, eager to go Kelly hunting. They had heard the report mentioned by Superintendent Sadlier in his telegram, and Superintendent Sadlier, having for his safety's sake placed the informant in the lock-up, questioned him closely. He was a bark stripper by occupation, somewhat intoxicated at the time, but he succeeded in convincing Mr Sadlier that he had seen the four bushrangers two days previously not far from Beechworth, "somewhere in the rocks, where it would take fifty men to get them out." In this neighbourhood, known as "Rat's Castle," resided the Byrnes and Sherritts, close friends of the outlaws, and though it was not certain at that time that Joe Byrne was one of them, Mr Sadlier thought the information worth vigorously acting upon.

Hence the telegram to Mr. Nicolson already quoted. The answer came promptly: "We are coming up as desired by special train. We shall leave about midnight. Meet us. Standish accompanies me." With Mr Nicolson's party were also, though his telegram did not mention it, two or three pressmen eager to be in anything that might be going.

Beechworth is distant by rail some fifty miles from Benalla, and the special train conveying Mr Standish, Mr Nicolson, the police, the tracker, and the Press, arrived at the latter place before daylight in the early morning. A great number of police and armed civilians were already gathered together ready mounted, and after a start had been made, about two miles out of Beechworth the cavalcade was still further augmented. Both the search parties with whom Mr Sadlier had endeavoured to communicate had received his message, and, thirteen men in all, they joined the party, which moved across country, like a squadron of cavalry, some fifty strong. The extraordinary part of the affair is that no one seems to have been in command. Mr Sadlier had organised the party. Mr Nicolson was chief Kelly-officer in command of the district, while Captain Standish was head of the Victorian Police, and among so many conflicting claims for leadership of the party, each officer seems to have resigned his own, tacitly assuming that the command had been taken by someone other than himself. All, however, apparently knew that they were proceeding towards Sherritt's hut, and, in no particular order, they advanced, crossing on their way some very rough country, great ranges of granite, with the result, says Mr Nicolson, that "the rumbling noise the party made was simply just like thunder, and the people heard us a mile off."

This was not a hopeful beginning for the capture of the outlaws. Mr Sadlier says the noise of shod horses in that country was unavoidable, but Mr Nicolson, who felt the want of discipline and the go-as-you-please nature of the affair very keenly, regarded it as a wild goose chase, and thought the police were only bringing ridicule upon themselves by the proceeding.

After crossing the range the party reached low ground again, and came in sight of a dwelling which they understood to be the Sherritts' hut. Up to this point Mr Nicolson did not even know where they were going beyond that they expected to find the Kellys somewhere in the vicinity. Mr Sadlier and Captain Standish had been talking together. Mr Nicolson busied himself in trying to knock the cavalcade into some kind of shape and grumbling about "the confounded noise," but now Mr Sadlier came up to him and said, "Mr Nicolson, this is the house of the Sherritts. The outlaws are said to be here." He continued to give some instructions, when Mr Nicolson took his turn at command, saying, "You send some men into that paddock"—there was a large paddock behind the house—"and see the men do not escape by the back." Then, turning to two or three men, and calling to them by name, Mr Nicolson ordered them to follow him, and galloped at full speed up to the front.

The object of the expedition had been to take the Kellys asleep. If they were still there they were doubtless by this time wakened by the thunderous noise of the cavalcade, and nothing was to be gained by delay. Accordingly, followed by his men, the police officer charged the house, flung himself from his horse at the door and broke it in. One of his party, Constable Bracken, tried to go first in the rush into the dwelling, but Mr Nicolson, resenting any attempt to precede him, thrust the constable aside, with the result that the gun carried by the later was exploded—the only shot fired upon the expedition, and one which created great excitement among the cordon of police surrounding the hut. Mr Nicolson's party searched it rapidly from room to room, but found not a soul.

Disappointed there, the police, riding on, reached another hut, which was rushed in the same manner, and though the Kellys were not there, a man, who was said that he had heard the party coming a mile away. A little further on, again, was the house of Mrs Byrne, mother of Joe Byrne, a member of the gang, and this house was empty like the others.

By this time day had broken some time, and the scanty population of the neighbourhood was astir. It took the police some time to satisfy themselves that none of the property of the murdered men was concealed in Mrs Byrne's hut, and when the search was over, there strolled up first to join the party a very fair and tall, high-shouldered young man, whom Constable Strahan introduced to his officers as Aaron Sherritt. "Here is a man," he said, "that knows the Kellys well, and will be of use to you; he knows all that is going on."

Certainly no one knew better, for Aaron Sherritt was an intimate, personal friend of Joe Byrne, and had been engaged in several horse-stealing exploits with him and the Kellys, besides which it was pretty certain that he had given them aid only a day or two before, when they were engaged, after the murders, on their attempt to cross the Murray. For a bushman he was something of a dandy, and physically a splendid specimen of a man. Mr Sadlier engaged him in conversation and presently consulted with Captain Standish and his other brother officer. In the meantime the men had dismounted from their horses.

Mrs. Byrne and her children appeared upon the scene, and some miners, who were prospecting and digging nearby came up and mingled with the throng. All idea of further Kelly hunting was abandoned for the day. Refreshments were sent for, and soon the incongruous gathering in the tableland valley resolved itself into a great impromptu early morning picnic. Captain Standish and Mr Sadlier, combining business with pleasure, immediately entered into negotiations with Aaron Sherritt, endeavouring to induce him to become a police agent and to betray his friends, the members of the gang. Mr Nicolson, who was still in a humour of stern disapproval with the whole affair, considered it very inadvisable to carry on conversation of such a kind in the presence, and, as he thought, in the hearing of constables and casual civilian spectators, and he even remonstrated with Captain Standish on the subject. It does not however appear from the evidence of this officer and Mr Sadlier, that the police, other than one or two who were treated confidentially, or any of the civilians present, knew anything of what was going on. They no doubt saw Sherritt speaking to the Commissioner, but the later most of the people did not know, and conversation between the police and an inhabitant of the locality was in any case natural enough.

The conversation was of an interesting kind. Certain proposals were made by Mr Sadlier to Sherritt, who was not satisfied with his authority to treat and was thereupon introduced to Captain Standish, and soon an arrangement was arrived at. Sherritt was very anxious that no harm should happen to Joe Byrne, and though Captain Standish was unable to promise that individual his liberty, he said he was sure his recommendation would be sufficiently weighty to secure Byrne's life, in the event of the gang being captured through Sherritt's instrumentality. With the guarantee to save Byrne's life Sherritt seemed satisfied. He was not to go with any party of police, but, pretending friendship with the gang and their allies, he was to take his own course as a secret agent—a calling which exposed him to the greatest possible danger should he be discovered—which in itself goes to prove that in his talk with the police officers he at least saw nothing compromising, in spite of the presence of the motley crowd. No money was given to him at the time, but it was understood that he was to receive payment for his services, beside which he would have shared in the large reward, ultimately reaching £8,000, offered by the Victorian Government for the capture of the outlaws. The interview with Sherritt being concluded, Captain Standish and Mr Sadlier then approached Mrs Byrne, whose hut was their temporary headquarters. They pointed out to her that her son had got his head into a halter, and that she could save him if she liked. However she was not amenable to argument. She probably was not impressed with the capacity of the police for effecting a capture, and her answer was, "He has made his bed, let him lie on it." The officers made use of all their persuasiveness, but entirely without effect, and they had to remain satisfied with Sherritt's promise of assistance as the outcome of their day's work at "Rats' Castle."

Here it may be remarked as a somewhat strange circumstance that though Byrne was evidently at this time known as a member of the gang, even his mother apparently admitting it, the sentence of outlawry was not passed against him for refusal to surrender at Mansfield on November 12, but against "a man whose name is unknown," of whom an elaborate description was given. The same method of address was also used to the fourth member of the gang, who afterwards proved to be Steve Hart, and, though definite knowledge of his identity was not obtained till a later period, even then those best qualified to judge had very little doubt about it. Two or three days previously Sergeant Steele, then under orders to proceed to Beechworth, had declared that the track taken under the One Mile Creek Railway Bridge near Wangaratta could only had been ventured upon, in the dangerously swollen state of the creek, by men who knew the banks well and who were fleeing for their lives, and he had named Steve Hart as almost certainly the daring guide who had led them.

At about eight o'clock, after having something to eat, the police party returned to Beechworth, sadly crestfallen and somewhat wearied by their night and morning under arms. The expedition had brought nothing but ridicule on the authorities, and from the outset was doomed to failure. Undoubtedly the Kellys had been in the neighbourhood a day or two before, but it was scarcely likely that they would allow themselves to be ridden down by a cavalry squadron, even had they not departed; and as a matter of fact, at the time of the expedition, sarcastically dubbed the "Charge of Sebastopol"—Sebastopol being the name of a locality close by—the Kellys were already securely in hiding in their familiar haunts of the Warby Ranges. Their security in this instance seems to have been owing less to their own activity than to the inactivity of Inspector Brooke Smith, which was of a most extraordinary kind. It will be remembered that to him, as officer in charge at Wangaratta, Sergeant Steele had trusted for the immediate pursuit of the men seen passing beneath the bridge. Constable Twomey, the man who conveyed the information to Steele, obtained it from a Mrs Delaney, who stated that at four o'clock on the Sunday morning she heard horses galloping and chains rattling, coming towards her house. She had horses running on the flat nearby, and thought "someone wanted to plant them." "I got up to the window," she said, "to see who they were, and saw four young men riding four horses. Two horses with two packs were in front, and four others running ahead of the men bareback." The horses seemed exhausted, and the riders were forcing them forward as best they could, being evidently anxious to get away from the vicinity of the town before daylight. They were going in the direction of the Warby Ranges, and Mrs. Delaney's son heard the noise of galloping over the wooden bridge which is the shortest way thither.

The police reported these things to Inspector Brooke Smith on November 4. They also told him, as further argument, that the men must be the Kellys; that no other persons would risk their lives by crossing the railway beneath a bridge under a dangerously swollen creek, when a railway crossing quite near was available for anyone not supremely anxious to avoid recognition.

In the face of these facts, Mr Smith remained idle until the 6th of the month. Then he set out for the ranges with a party from Wangaratta. It came upon the outlaws' tracks, recovered Kennedy's pack horse, which they had abandoned, and then, by his orders, returned to Wangaratta. A fresh start was to be made at 4 a.m. next morning, but after waiting for their officer till seven the men were compelled to set out without him. He followed, and catching them up, caused unnecessary delay by insisting on making detours to follow tracks; and, in short, seems to have justified the finding of the Police Commission, "that he was determined that his party should not overtake the outlaws," and that "what renders his action all the more reprehensible is the fact that upon no other occasion throughout the pursuit, from the murders at the Wombat to the final affray at Glenrowan, was there presented a more favourable prospect of capturing the gang."

8
THE OUTLAWS LOST TO SIGHT

IN consequence of his feeble action in conducting the chase after the outlaws referred to in the last chapter, Mr Brooke Smith was sent by Mr Nicolson to Beechworth, with instructions to attend to ordinary police duty and meddle no more in the Kelly business. Mr Smith, among other disqualifications as leader of a search party, seemed to have a constitutional inability to leave his bed before eight or nine o'clock in the morning, and an unconquerable aversion to remaining out of it under rough camp conditions at night. Mr Nicolson himself had to rouse Mr. Smith on one occasion and send him after the men he should have been leading upon the tracks of the outlaws. There were black trackers at Wangaratta, one an old man from Corranderrk aboriginal station who still retained some of the cunning of his early days of hunting life, and a young man, Jemmy, whom the old one called his pupil, but who did not credit to his teaching, being a stupid, useless fellow.

In addition to Kennedy's packhorse Mr Brooke Smith's party had picked up a ramrod, very probably dropped by the outlaws; but owing to the delay before pursuit took place Mr. Nicolson did not think the men were ever really very close upon the Kellys. An examination of Kennedy's horse led him to the conclusion that it had been abandoned for about a week.

Having sent Mr Brooke Smith to remain out of mischief at Beechworth, Mr Nicolson took matters in hand himself, and on November 11, the day before that upon which the outlaws were invited to surrender themselves at Mansfield, a report came in that they had been seen crossing the railway line near Glenrowan, a township about nine miles on the Melbourne side of Wangaratta, and about five miles from Greta, which lies to the east of the railway line connecting the two first-named places. The informant was a platelayer who said the Kellys had crossed from Greta towards the Warby Ranges side, and accordingly Mr Sadlier and Mr Nicolson, meeting at Glenrowan, started at daylight on November 12, with some constables and the two trackers already mentioned. The tracks were perfectly plain and the blacks led the party to the foot of the ranges. There, though according to Mr Sadlier the tracks were still visible going on into the bush, the blacks insisting upon turning aside and leading the party into marshy ground, where there were thousands of prints of horse and cattle hoofs and it was quite out of the question to follow any individual tracks. All the cattle of the neighbourhood came to this spot to water, but it was impossible to get the black trackers back on to the original trail, undoubtedly because it was leading to cover where an ambush might be expected. From fear and cunning the blacks resolutely refused to go first, and the police were unable to take the lead, since by so doing they would spoil the tracks and made them impossible for the blacks to follow, while the constables themselves would be quite incapable of keeping upon them after they left the soft ground at the foot of the ranges.

However, the police did their best, striking out in different directions for themselves and still hoping to pick up a good trail, until by some mistake a small party under Sergeant Steele got out of sight while the others were waiting for luncheon. Mr Sadleir heard it afterwards reported as coming from Ned Kelly that he was concealed nearby, saw the police party, and could, if he had chosen, easily have shot Mr Nicolson and Mr Sadleir from where he sat. No proof was forthcoming of the truth or falsehood of this statement, but at any rate it is clear that from some source Kelly had most accurate information of the disposition of the police party, for he described how the members of it sat in a little open space where there was water, mentioned some of the men present, and described the brands upon their horses.

With good black trackers the officers believed they would have had a very fair chance of bringing the matter to an issue; but, as it was, they found it hopeless to attempt any further move and were forced to return to Benalla.

Mr Sadleir at this time was only just convalescent from rheumatic fever, and still so weak that his medical man declared it highly dangerous for him to go out upon search parties and suffer exposure from the weather and cold night air of the hills. Therefore, after this attempt to come up with the outlaws, he did not personally engage in the chase for some considerable time, but, attending to office duties, left the more active work to Mr Nicolson who was indefatigable in his efforts. For the next few weeks there was more searching than chasing, for no definite news came to hand of the Kellys' whereabouts, but all the North-Eastern District was parcelled out into areas whereon parties of police varying in number from six to nine were constantly on the move, scouring the country by day and camping out by night.

With many of these parties Mr Nicolson went in person, and for a man of his age the work was most arduous. All the police officers engaged, in fact, were well on in years, Mr Nicolson being close on fifty, Mr Hare forty-eight, and Mr Sadlier forty-five, while they all had done active and often most severe duty for more than twenty-five years in the Victorian police force.

Describing his general experience of the search party work, Mr Nicolson spoke as follows: "After travelling through the ranges and that country, where we would come to a halting place, we were in the habit of camping first and having tea and placing sentries and having supper, and would then select a place to sleep in, leaving the fire, of which we had very little, and moving on to another place to sleep. I then, instead of being able to lie down to rest with the men at the time, generally had to go with two or three men to places from one to four miles off on foot—huts of suspected persons, and so on. . . I would not get back to the camp after visiting those places until above twelve or two or three o'clock at night. I had to lie down to rest till daybreak, which at this time (November) was very early. This had a serious effect upon me. It reduced my strength. It also affected the whole party; we would come in very much fagged—horses and men. The young men used to recuperate in a couple of days, but it took me, at my time of life, and the other members of the force, mounted constables and others, more than that, but I had to go out notwithstanding at once."

In addition to the fatigue and hardship occasioned by these expeditions, which Mr Nicolson says were the most severe he had undergone since joining the police force, was the mortifying consciousness that the district residents were ever more ready to frustrate than to forward the plans of the searchers.

They could not get guides and no assistance, save from one man named Dickson, of Wangaratta, who subsequently joined the force, and another named Nicholson, from Mansfield, who did good service. There were three secret agents, more or less trusted; but these could never show themselves openly with the police, and an endeavour was always made to keep the starting of every expedition a secret, which, however, was difficult, and whenever a party left headquarters, the news of it was immediately noised throughout the district, creating a sensation among the well-disposed inhabitants and putting the outlaws on their guard. Consequently, party after party, having spent various times from a few days to a fortnight in the bush or the mountains, returned wearied out to their different stations.

Up to this time no use had been made of the Felons Apprehension Act, which took effect from November 12 and gave the police very wide powers in arresting people known to have concealed or in any way succoured the outlaws.

Sympathisers were known in plenty, but the difficulty was to obtain proof of any act committed by them in contravention of the law. It was quite certain, for instance, that Mrs Skillion, the sister of the Kellys, was in the habit of conveying food to the gang, and it was observed that far more bread was baked at her residence at Greta that could possibly be accounted for by the wants of her family. On November 15 the prisoner Williamson, concerned together with the Kellys in the attack of Constable Fitzpatrick, and then in Pentridge Prison, furnished Inspector Green with his ideas of the localities likely to be frequented by the Kellys and their most probable associates. The places he mentioned were the more or less inaccessible heads of various creeks and rivers, some of them forty miles apart, from which places, as Williamson admitted, the outlaws could see the police coming; so the information was not of much value. The police themselves were aware that any one of those places might be chosen as a hiding place, but the trouble was to know which would be favoured at any particular time. Williamson was, however, confident that the Kellys would obtain rations from Mrs Skillion, and he mentioned that she would signal to them by hanging a white sheet, when police were about, on a sapling near her house, which could be seen from a great distance.

Another prisoner, named Williams, also an associate of the Kellys, on October 29 had informed Inspector Green that the outlaws carried with them a small tent and about a month's rations. He too mentioned their favoured haunts, and laid stress on the probable endeavours of Mrs Skillion to assist them. In particular he described the position and appearance of a hollow log near her residence, in which he expected food would be planted for the Kellys or their associates to carry away. Search was made for this log and it was found; but from its appearance the police concluded particular watch upon it, for which they were afterwards blamed by the Police Commission. It is probable, however, that the log was not then actually in use. The Kellys and their friends had no doubt availed themselves of it during some of the numerous bygone periods when they were in hiding from justice, and the mere fact that several others beside themselves knew of its history was likely to put them on their guard.

But whatever were the facts concerning the log, the police had no doubt that Mrs Skillion was conveying food, either by herself or confederates, to the outlaws, and they tried hard to ascertain what became of the great bakings turned out from her oven, with the result that they soon learnt from a reliable agent that she used frequently to ride away from her house in the middle of the night carrying a well-filled swag. Several attempts were made to follow her, but they all failed. On the face of it one would suppose that here was a chance of effecting a capture, but

Mr Sadlier insisted that to follow Mrs Skillion for any distance of horseback, which would be necessary since she rode herself, was impossible without being discovered. If she cantered she would get out of sight, and would soon hear the hoof beats of any horse following her when she pulled up to a walk again, at what distance ahead of them the pursuers could not tell. Wherever Mrs Skillion went, she went far, for according to the agents' information her horse was always knocked up when she returned, and for her expeditions she constantly used fresh mounts. Had her trail been followed by black trackers some news might have resulted, but there were no competent and trustworthy aboriginals in Victoria at that time, and even later, when the Queensland Government offered to send some of theirs to Victoria, Captain Standish, who had little faith in their usefulness, refused the offer of their assistance. Another alternative possible, and perhaps of value, would have been and perhaps of value, would have been the arrest of Mrs Skillion under the Felons Apprehension Act, and later, in case of her making signals from her house as Williamson suggested she would do, Captain Standish urged the advisability of her arrest. Nevertheless, at this time, for several reasons nothing was done. For one thing Mr Nicolson did not consider there was sufficient evidence against her to secure a conviction, and further it was hoped that immunity from interference would lead her and her brothers to betray themselves by more daring undertakings beneath the noses of the police. The agents at any moment were likely to give definite and fresh information which might enable a sudden blow to be struck, and therefore, fully aware that the Kellys were being provisioned and interviewed almost in sight of the police, the officers felt themselves compelled to suffer these things, and to remain more or less inactive in the hope of some really good chance arising for an successful attempt at arrest.

9
MR WYATT AND THE BROKEN WIRES

FOR some weeks after Mr Nicolson's and Mr Sadlier's expedition on which the black trackers shirked duty, although many conflicting rumours of the Kellys' doings reached the police nothing authentic was reported, and the time was devoted to search parties on no particular information, such as Mr Nicolson described.

The prisoner Williamson, who seemed to have access to some mysterious fund of knowledge, gave warning to Inspector Green that the gang might be expected to raid one of the banks in some North-Eastern township, and mentioned in particular Seymour, which is only about sixty miles from Melbourne, and considerably south of the district known as the Kelly country, in which the bushrangers were most at home. There is some conflict in the evidence as to whether Mr Nicolson got express notice of this warning. Captain Standish afterwards claimed that he did, and in fact that Mr Nicolson mentioned it to him. Accordingly the Commissioner, leaving Mr Nicolson to take measures on his own account, spoke specially to Mr Hare, who, though resident in Melbourne, had charge of the police district immediately adjoining the North-Eastern, and including Seymour within its limits. Acting on Captain Standish's instructions Mr Hare took measures to give considerable extra police protection to Seymour and all other townships up the railway line as far as Avenel, beyond which the stations were under Mr Nicolson's charge, and Mr Hare also warned the managers of the banks that there was likelihood of a raid being made upon them. More police had been applied for by Mr Sadleir and Mr Nicolson for the work of pursuing the outlaws, but both of them assert that they had no word of expected danger to the banks, and therefore no special measures were taken to avert it.

Mrs Skillion's long expeditions had led them to suppose that the Kellys were hidden away deep in the mountains, intent upon nothing but evading pursuit, and the police saw good cause to believe from such reports as reached them that the gang was about to make another attempt to escape into New South Wales. Among the men who gave Mr Nicolson real or fanciful accounts of what the Kellys were doing was one Patrick Quin, husband of Ned Kelly's aunt, and himself a relative to the outlaws; and he claims to have given warning of an intention on their part to stick up one of the banks, but this Mr Nicolson denies, and adds that, coming from such a source, he would in any case have given little weight to the information.

Thus, without any further developments, weeks passed by until Monday, December 9, when Patrick Quin, the man mentioned above, came into the barracks yard at Benalla just after Mr Nicolson and party had returned from a search expedition in the direction of Mansfield, and asserted that he had very important information. This information was to the effect that the Kellys were living in a basin among the hills on the King River, in wild country some seventy miles from Benalla, far beyond Glenmore, the residence of another Quin, close to which the bushranger, Power, had been captured by Mr Nicolson and Mr Hare many years before. Quin wished Mr Nicolson to meet him near this basin on the following night, but Mr Nicolson, having no reason to trust the man, refused, pointing to the jaded state of his horses, and asking how it was possible to travel them another seventy miles within a few hours of their return. He had consulted with Mr Sadlier, and believed, as after events proved to be the case, that the offer to meet the police on the King River was merely an attempt to put them off the track.

Sometime previously Senior-Constable Kelly had forwarded from Hedi, an outlaying station on the King River about thirty-five miles from Benalla, a letter which had fallen into his hands, apparently revealing a plan on behalf of certain persons to assist the outlaws in leaving the district and crossing the Murray into New South Wales. The opinion of all the respectable portion of the community gave further weight to the view held by Mr Nicolson and Mr Sadlier, that the Kellys, baffled in their former attempt by the floods, would try again to cross the river, and the letter helped them in deciding to act. This document, which was addressed to a near blood relation of the Kellys and one of their most thorough assistants, ran as follows:

"Sir, I have been requested by E. and D. Kelly to do what I could to assist them in crossing here" (the letter was not dated as to time or place). I am to write to you to let you know the arrangements. They are to be at a time to be named at the junction of Indigo Creek and Murray, and there is to be a password, it is this—'Any work to be had?' 'Yes!' 'Where?' On the New South Wales side one shall meet you. I will have a boat ready. There must not be any horses come to the river; if you should have horses they must be led by the bridge to a safe place already prepared for them. I will have four on each side of the river to watch upper and lower side. I have a place fixed where you will be safe. If you should want horses there will be some got for you. There are two say they will join you if requested. You must mind it will want money and I have got none. When you write, direct to Howlong for—(the singer)."

Mr Sadlier, after the destruction of the gang, did not think it wise to mention the name of the writer, who was well known and suspected in the neighbourhood, but the envelope showed the postmarks of Bungowunnah and Albury—border towns—of December 3. Half believing this information, but with a note to the effect that no action by the writer or his confederates was to be apprehended for a few days, unless the letter were a blind to cover other movements, Mr Sadleir sent word of it to the police- sergeant near Howlong, at the junction of the Murray and Indigo rivers, between Albury and Bungowunnah where the proposed crossing was to take place, and he also sent notice to the New South Wales police.

Then, on Mr Nicolson's return from the search expedition, the two officers, consulting together, agreed that it was most desirable to have a good watch kept upon all Murray crossings in the suspected neighbourhood and decided to go up themselves to Albury to direct matters in person.

Accordingly Mr Nicolson on December 10 telegraphed to the officer in charge at Albury asking him to meet him that evening. He telegraphed also to the Commissioner, informing him of the move, and he and Mr Sadlier at eight o'clock in the evening went down to the railway station to take the Sydney train for the border. On the platform they met Mr Wyatt, a police magistrate for the North-Eastern District, and noticed immediately that he was in a most excited state. He appeared to be concealing something beneath his coat, and, calling to Mr Nicolson to accompany him, he rushed into the nearest room on the railway station, which proved to be the ladies' waiting room, and, as he himself said, he felt very much shocked at the necessity of excluding ladies from it. However, he closed the door and did so, also excluding Mr Sadlier, who employed himself unsuccessfully in trying to discover from the railway officials the cause of the excitement while Mr Wyatt communicated his news to Mr Nicolson. It was to the effect that the telegraph wires were broken down between Euroa and Violet Town, apparently cut with some sharp instrument, and Mr Wyatt believed it was the work of the Kellys. In support of his statement he showed Mr Nicolson several broken ends of the wires, which he had obtained earlier in the day from the place where the smash had occurred. Mr Wyatt and Mr Nicolson presently issued from the room and for a minute or two the conversation continued, Mr Wyatt asking the police officers if his news would alter their plans. He was in an extremely perturbed state, and his want of calmness did not impress Mr Nicolson with the weight of his communication, more especially as the guard and the driver of the train assured him that there was nothing wrong—a circumstance arising from the fact that Mr Wyatt, in his zeal for the public welfare, had given them the most emphatic orders not to create any alarm. If questioned about the broken telegraph line, they were to say, "It looks like a whirlwind;" and unfortunately Mr Wyatt neglected to make an exception of the police officers when he urged the railway men to preserve a calm and unconcerned demeanour to everybody. His own evident perturbation did something to atone, but he himself also forgot in the hurried conversation to supply Mr Nicolson with several important details which might have affected the police officer's judgment. The result was that to Mr Wyatt's question, "Will this alter your plans?" Mr Nicolson replied, "No; it will not alter them;" and with Mr Sadlier he entered the train and proceeded on the journey to Albury.

The whole conversation had taken very few minutes. Telegraph lines were frequently broken in that district. No one but Mr Wyatt seemed to have an inkling of anything wrong. The police officers were on what they considered an important quest, and even had the Kellys cut the wires it might very well have been to prevent reports of their flight across the Murray reaching Melbourne.

It was unfortunate that Mr Wyatt was not more explicit, for he had really important news beyond the breaking of the wires to impart. Going by luggage train from Violet Town to Euroa on that day, December 10, shortly after the train left the station he was addressed by a telegraph repairer named Watt, from Benalla, who came along the foot plate and told him the wires were down.

Mr Wyatt and Watt agreed to keep a look out on either side of the train, and about eight miles from Violet Town, and three and three-quarters from Euroa, which is on the south of Melbourne side, Mr Wyatt saw that a considerable length of wire and six posts were down. This was opposite a station homestead named Faithfull's Creek, which lies in full view of and only a few hundred yards from the railway line. Watt came again along the footplate to Mr Wyatt, telling him it was impossible to mend the line without further material and assistance, and asking Mr Wyatt to send a message for him to Melbourne. Then, the train slowing down, Watt jumped off the footplate and the train went on to Euroa, while the repairer walked towards the Faithfull's Creek homestead.

On arriving at Euroa, Mr Wyatt gave Watt's message concerning the requisite aid and material very fully to Mr Gorman, the stationmaster, and informed him that the line was "down through a whirlwind." This was Mr Wyatt's own opinion, strengthened by that of some passengers whom he had heard say that no men could have pulled the posts down like that—that it would require at least a team of bullocks to do it.

From the station Mr Wyatt went straight to the courthouse, distant about half a mile, where his business, which consisted in granting a few licences, was over in a quarter of an hour. Being still much interested in the question of the broken wires, Mr Wyatt obtained a horse and buggy—with some difficulty, since nearly all the horse-flesh and vehicles of the township were under requisition for a large funeral then proceeding—and drove out towards Faithfull's Creek. Near the homestead he encountered a man who asked him if that were the road to the station, to which Mr Wyatt replied he did not know, and the stranger, making use of some obscene expression, rode away. Looking at his watch, Mr Wyatt came to the conclusion that with this slow going horse, which objected to any pace faster than a walk, it would be impossible for him to go further and yet be back in time to catch the Sydney train northwards from Euroa, as he had to do to keep an appointment at another station next day, and he therefore returned to Euroa. On the way a strong suspicion flashed across his mind that the man who had accosted him was one of the outlaws, and as he jogged stationwards the idea that the destruction of the line was the work of the Kellys gradually gained strength. He remembered that within hundreds of yards of the fallen telegraph posts were no fallen trees or branches, which effectually disposed of the whirlwind theory. On again meeting Mr Gorman his first question was as to whether the repairer Watt had returned. The stationmaster said, "No;" whereon, remarking that the distance was only three miles and three-quarters and that Watt could not repair the line himself, Mr Wyatt told his suspicions. "Mr Gorman," he said, "there is something up; you must give me express permission to ride upon the engine and stop the train and get down to examine the line. I do not believe it was a whirlwind now, because I recollect there was not a single tree or shrub injured anywhere about." He particularly enjoined Mr Gorman to tell no one of what he suspected, and said to him, "To anybody who enquires, answer, 'It looks like a whirlwind.'"

Permission to ride on the engine was granted by Mr Gorman, and Mr Wyatt left shortly afterwards by the train going north towards Benalla. Though evening was coming on it was still daylight when the train reached Faithfull's Creek, and was stopped for Mr Wyatt to jump off the engine. The guard of the train also alighted, and between them, he and Mr Wyatt finding both the Government and the railway's telegraph wires in a hopeless tangle, and satisfying themselves that they were cut and not broken, twisted off and brought away with them a number of the ends as evidence of the fact. To the guard Mr Wyatt said, " It is clear the line is cut. I believe the Kellys are about. Say not a word to the passengers or anyone, but say as I told the driver and fireman and Gorman to say, that it looks like a whirlwind." To the passengers who made enquiry, Mr. Wyatt replied with his diplomatic formula: "The line is down and it looks like a whirlwind."

At Violet Town, the next station, Mr Wyatt told the stationmaster to say nothing to passengers or other people, but to telegraph to Melbourne that the line was down, which could be done in spite of the break in the wires by sending the message northward to Albury, whence it could go to Denilquin in New South Wales, and southward by another line to Melbourne.

From Violet Town to Benalla is a distance of sixteen miles, and at the latter place, when the train arrived at seven o'clock, Mr Wyatt met and talked with Mr Nicolson as already described. Unfortunately he made no mention of Watt's failure to return from his inspection, and said nothing of the man who had used bad language to him at Faithfull's Creek, nor did he succeed in conveying to the police officers his own certainty that the Kellys were in the neighbourhood, while his precautions as to secrecy had been so efficacious that from the guard and fireman Mr Sadlier could get not a word beyond, "It looks like a whirlwind." Later on, after some scruples as to whether he should interfere with police plans, Mr Wyatt, who remained at Benalla, wired to Captain Standish the news that the lines were broken and that Mr Nicolson and Mr Sadlier had gone on to Wangaratta. To a constable named Whelan he told his suspicions, and finding Whelan much impressed by them, asked if he could provide a special train to return to Faithfull's Creek. Whelan had no authority himself to order a special train, but wired asking for it both to Captain Standish in Melbourne and Mr Nicolson in Albury, and finally a telegram arrived from the former in consequence of which at 1.30 a.m. a train started southward, carrying Mr Wyatt, armed and eager for fight, and Senior Constable Johnson, Detective Ward, Constable Whelan, one or two other constables, black trackers and horses. Mr Wyatt rode on the engine, keeping a lookout with powerful field glasses lest the railway line should be injured, but without accident the train pulled up opposite Faithfull's Creek. From the homestead two men were seen approaching, and the occupants of the train found that one of of them was Mr McCauley, manager of the station. They had a sensational tale to tell of the late presence of the Kellys at Faithfull's Creek, which fully justified all Mr Wyatt's alarm. He delayed the train for about half an hour to take the men's depositions to be forwarded for the use of Captain Standish, after which, since horses could not be taken out of the trucks away from a platform, the train started again and in a few minutes reached Euroa where matters were considered concerning the pursuit.

10
THE STICKING-UP OF FAITHFULL'S CREEK

FAITHFULL'S Creek Station homestead, standing as it does in full sight of a main railway line and close to the old Sydney Road, less than four miles distant from a busy township, was the last place at which the Kellys might be expected to make a sudden appearance, and the gang's exploit there was one of the most daring and picturesque in their career. On December 9 all had gone as usual till after midday. George Stephens, a groom, and Fitzgerald, another employe, were then at their dinner in the kitchen, where was also Mrs Fitzgerald, the station housekeeper, busying herself about the men's meal, when a roughly dressed, bearded man, coming to the door, inquired if Mr McCauley, the station manager, was at home. On being told that he was not, the stranger walked away, saying he would wait, and Stephens went down to the stables, whereupon the man came back, and introduced himself to Mrs Fitzgerald as Ned Kelly. By this time he had been joined by three other men in charge of four horses, three bays and a grey, in excellent condition, and Ned Kelly politely informing Fitzgerald and his wife who they were, gave his assurance that he and his mates intended no harm, but must have food for themselves and their horses. Mrs Fitzgerald accepted the position philosophically and pointed out the stable to Kelly, who, going down there with Fitzgerald and one of his mates, found Stephens and another man whom Fitzgerald pointed out to Kelly. The bushranger stood without speaking for a moment or two at the stable door, where the men did not take much notice of him. Then turning to Stephens with a smile, "I suppose you don't know who I am," he said, in evident anticipation of effecting a sensational surprise.

"Perhaps you are Ned Kelly," was the quiet answer given at random, to which Kelly, decidedly annoyed, replied that Stephens "seemed to be a —— good guesser." At the same time he produced a revolver, and, mollified by Stephens' saying that he was only joking, he explained that the horses of the gang must be stabled and fed.

While this matter was being attended to, Kelly conversed with Stephens in the stable, and gave his own version of the shooting of the police, which chiefly differed from McIntyre's in so far as he asserted that Lonigan, Scanlon, and Kennedy had all three showed fight and fired several shots before they met their deaths. Lonigan, according to Kelly, had taken shelter behind a pile of logs and opened fire from there, being shot through the head when he rose to take aim. Scanlon had fired himself, and been shot in his turn before dismounting, while Kennedy had taken shelter behind his horse and made excellent revolver practice, one bullet going through Kelly's beard , another grazing his ribs, and a third touching Dan on the shoulder. The sergeant had then, Kelly said, made a running fight of it from tree to tree, till Kelly had shot him twice— once in the shoulder, and once through the chest, after which he fell. Either from vainglorious pride in his shooting powers or from a desire to shield his mates, should they ever be captured, Ned Kelly asserted that no one but he had taken any part in the killing of the police. Murder he declared it was not, but a necessary act of self-defence against men who had come out determined to shoot him.

Stephens was afterwards escorted by Kelly from the stable and confined with others in the store-room, a wooden slab building, about twenty yards distant from the house. The plan of the outlaws, though daring in the extreme, was very simple, and consisted in the occupation of the station as a base of operations, where they themselves and their horses might gain rest and food before attempting the other coup which they had planned. The confinement of the station hands gave them very little trouble. One by one, as they dropped in, they were encountered by one of the gang, who presented a loaded revolver at their heads and told them the station was stuck up and that they were prisoners. There was no difficulty in adding them to the gradually increasing crowd in the store-room, which was an easy room to guard, since the door and windows, close together, could be watched by one or more of the outlaws heavily armed with loaded rifle and revolvers.

Several prisoners were collected during the day, and at five o'clock, when the manager, Mr McCauley, rode in from an outstation he had been visiting, the wonderful quietness and deserted appearance of the place greatly surprised him, but a warning word, with advice to surrender, was called out to him by Fitzgerald as he approached the store. His inclination to treat the matter as a stupid jest was quickly dispelled by the appearance of Kelly with a revolver from behind the building, and seeing no help for it, he suffered himself, too, to be made a prisoner. At first the Kellys, keeping a watch on Mr McCauley, allowed him freedom of movement, and he suggested that everyone might as well be as comfortable as circumstances permitted and have some tea. The women of the place had not been shut up or molested, and they prepared a meal, of which the Kellys as well as the prisoners partook, the later taking the precaution to make others eat first in case the food should be poisoned.

Only two of the outlaws sat down at one time while the others stood by with their revolvers in their hands to prevent mischief.

Towards evening another visitor arrived, a draper named Gloster who resided at Seymour but was then hawking some of his goods through the country. He knew the station, where he had previously done business, and determining to pitch his camp there for the night, he left a young man named Beecroft in charge of his covered wagon and horses which had been unharnessed on the road, and went to the kitchen to get a billy of boiling water for his tea. As he was returning to the waggon a man called him back, saying the station was stuck up, but Gloster took no notice and went on to his camp, which was promptly visited by Ned and Dan Kelly, the former in a very bad temper. Gloster had just climbed into his cart to get a pistol which he kept there, when he found revolvers pointed at his head from either side by the outlaws and was roughly ordered to come down, which he did, but he went on making preparations for his supper. Ned Kelly had a pair of handcuffs in one hand and a revolver in the other. When asked by the hawker who he was and what right he had to interfere, the outlaw replied in his usual modest style: "I am Ned Kelly, and a better man never stepped in two shoes."

This was by no means Gloster's first encounter with bushrangers, as he had been stuck up twice before, and on one occasion shot in the shoulder by the man named Daly. It appears that he now ran very considerable risk of being shot again, owing to his obstinacy and slowness in surrendering himself. Dan Kelly was very anxious to "put a bullet through the wretch," but Mr McCauley, who had accompanied the outlaws to the cart, joined in urging him to bail up, and at last seeing the hopelessness of resisting, he confessed that there was in his waggon a revolver which Kelly secured. He was then led with Beecroft to the kitchen, where he was allowed to have supper under surveillance and afterwards locked up with the other men in the store.

There was not much sleep for the prisoners that night. One or two of the outlaws kept guard outside and Ned Kelly remained with them in the store, which was ill ventilated and inconveniently crowded, talking much and boastfully of what he had done and was going to do. Many of the men asked him questions, but they were all most careful to avoid the word "murder" in speaking of the death of the police. Kelly confirmed the story that he had shot Kennedy when he was lying wounded on the ground, in order, he said, to put him out of his misery, and he added that, having respect for Kennedy as a brave man, he had covered the body with a cloak. The rumour that he had cut off one of the sergeant's ears he protested was a lie. The police, Kelly declared, had persecuted him and all his family, who were innocent in the matter of Fitzpatrick, and they were, he said, his natural enemies; but on his own showing he had done a good deal to make enemies of them, since he confessed to having stolen 280 horses in his time.

Before going to bed for the night the Kellys allowed the prisoners out under guard to get a few breaths of fresh air, and then locked them up again. As to the projected robbery of the bank at Euroa the outlaws appear to have made no secret, and very early in the morning they were on watch for any persons who might approach the station, and who were to be shut up with the others in order to prevent their departing and giving the alarm.

The first haul was of a shooting party of three Melbourne gentlemen—one riding and the others driven by a resident of the district in a spring cart which approached the station in the morning. The sportsmen had just returned from the Strathbogie Ranges where they had spent some days in shooting kangaroo and other game. On the road near the house they were stopped by Kelly and one of his mates, who informed them that the station was stuck up, and told them to turn their horses round. They immediately got out of the cart which contained the guns, a rifle and some ammunition, and the rider approaching, when he heard that the station was stuck up, suggested that they should jump into the cart and get the guns. This proposal was sternly negatived by Ned Kelly. He saw that the party did not know him and amused himself by accusing Mr Casement, the owner of the cart, of being Ned Kelly and of having stolen the vehicle. This accusation was vehemently denied by the sportsmen, several of whom were Scotch; and supposing the outlaws to be plain- clothes policemen, they declared they were honest men, and asked if the Kellys were about, to which Ned said "yes." They protested strongly against being interfered with, and one of them went so far as to threaten Ned Kelly, who had said something about putting handcuffs on him, that he would report him to his superior officer.

Still supposing the outlaws to be particularly ill- mannered policemen—Ned Kelly had threatened to blow Mr Dudley's brains out if he gave any more cheek—Mr McDougal, Mr Tennant, Mr Dudley, and Mr Casement, the gentlemen of the shooting party, allowed themselves to be conducted under protest to the homestead, where the little comedy was brought to a close by Stephens, the groom, formally introducing the outlaw as Mr. Edward Kelly. The prisoners were then searched by Dan Kelly and locked up with the others in the store-room, where Ned Kelly became conversational with them also, and among other favours, showed them the gold watch which he had taken from Kennedy. The rifle, guns and ammunition in the shooting party's cart were all confiscated, but beyond imprisonment the men suffered no violence, while the women were still allowed to remain free and were interfered with in no way, though Dan did suggest having a lark with them—a proposal promptly squelched by his elder brother.

Four trains passed the house before half-past two in the afternoon—two each way—and when they were heard approaching, the prisoners were commanded to keep very quiet, with the promise that anyone who raised an alarm would have his brains blown out. About half-past two the outlaws went on to the railway line, and worked the destruction to the telegraph lines which had excited Mr Wyatt, and while thus engaged they encountered four railway gangers, who were arrested and added to the squad of prisoners in the store-room.

A little after three Ned Kelly, Dan Kelly and Steve Hart dressed themselves for an expedition to Euroa and made all necessary arrangements. The capture of the hawker's cart was a particularly useful circumstance to them, as making a selection from the wardrobe it contained, they dressed themselves most carefully in brand new clothes, and did not even neglect such refinements as the use of scent, to which they helped themselves liberally from Mr. Gloster's bottles. *En-passant* it may be remarked that, though they made it a boast that they never robbed poor men, and though they refused small sums of money which were offered them by some of the prisoners, the outlaws made Gloster no payment for some £14 worth of wearing apparel which they took away with them, nor for the revolver which he valued at £3 10s.

Having got ready for the journey they requested Mr McCauley to write a small cheque for presentation by them at the Euroa bank, and then taking their horses from the stable turned them loose in the paddock. At half-past three they set out from the station, Ned Kelly driving Gloster's cart which was a hooded vehicle, Dan Kelly taking the spring cart belonging to the shooting party, and Steve Hart riding one of the station horses, while his own was left to graze in the home paddock.

Byrne was left behind in sole charge of the thirty prisoners which by this time the store-room contained. It was seemingly a large order for one man to control them; but, stuck all over with revolvers and with a double barrelled gun in his hand, and two loaded rifles within easy reach, Byrne calmly marched up and down before the door, apparently in no way overpowered by his responsibility. There was, in fact, not very ardent desire on the part of the prisoners to escape. They were cramped and uncomfortable, but this, not to speak of any impersonal desire of bringing the scoundrels to justice, was by no means strong enough inducement to make them risk their lives in an attack upon Joe Byrne. There were axes in the hut. One or two daring spirits did suggest that they should chop their way out and rush upon the outlaw. Doubtless he might have been overcome and captured; but doubtless also one or more men would have lost their lives in the attempt, which prevented any enthusiasm for the idea. Among those who might otherwise have been in favour of some bold step there was also the knowledge that the store-room contained strong sympathisers with the Kellys as well as bona fide prisoners, and it was also suspected that other of the outlaws' friends were lurking in hiding near the station. Accordingly Joe Byrne was not threatened in any way while he mounted guard over his prisoners.

Once, when a passing train slowed down and came almost to a standstill in front of the station, must have been an exciting time for the prisoners and an anxious one for Byrne, who might reasonably have expected an attack. However, he showed no sight for faltering. The train was that in which Mr Wyatt travelled to Euroa when he and the telegraph repairer, Watt, first observed the break in the wires. Watt, as related, jumped off the engine, while the train quickened pace again and went on. After a casual examination of the damage Watt walked up towards the homestead to ask for information and assistance. As he approached the store-room, Byrne, covering him with a gun, ordered him to come forward, which he was forced to do, and he, too, was locked up with the ever growing crowd in the store-room. Thus the non-appearance of the line repairer, in the event, afforded the fullest justification of Mr Wyatt's suspicion that his failure to return to Euroa argued something very wrong at Faithfull's Creek. The curious matter was, that at the very moment he was pouring forth these suspicions to Mr Gorman, something far more wrong was in progress only half a mile from where he stood.

The Euroa Bank Robbery.—

11
THE EUROA BANK ROBBERY

Proceeding quietly along the road the bushrangers reached Euroa without incident, and pulled up at the National Bank, a one-storied building, which lay, very conveniently for their purpose, on the side of the township nearest to Faithfull's Creek, but of course in no way isolated from the rest of the buildings. The principal hotel, in fact, was distant not more than forty yards, and the bank was also in sight of the railway station. It so happened that a large number of residents were absent from Euroa at a funeral outside the town, while others were interested in the licensing business going on at the court half a mile away, and these things helped to account for the two carts driving unobserved up to the bank door. Had anyone seen them they would scarcely have attracted notice, for the gang were all most respectably dressed. Gloster's cart, with his name painted on it, was well known in Euroa, and Kelly had taken with him Gloster's boy to hold the horses, while he pursued his business at the bank.

He and Hart commenced operations by knocking at the bank door, which was shut, as the bank closed at three and it was then after office hours. In answer to an enquiry concerning their business, Kelly said that he had a cheque of Mr McCauley's, which he wanted cashed. Without opening the door one of the clerks told him he was too late, but Kelly begged for admission, saying that he would be greatly inconvenienced if he did not obtain the cash that night, whereupon Mr Bradley, the teller, partially opened the door, and Kelly and Hart, forcing their way in, shut the door behind them.

In the office they found Mr Bradley and another clerk, Mr Booth, both of whom, with revolvers presented at their heads, found themselves unable to resist. Ned Kelly mentioned his name and explained the object of his visit, demanding all the cash the bank contained. A large amount was on the teller's table or in the drawers, having been in use that day, but Kelly wanted the contents of the strong room as well, and, driving the clerks before them, he and Hart, with a revolver in each hand, made their way into the manager's room, which opened from the main office. There they found Mr Scott, the manager, who was unable to secure his revolver before he was made to hold his hands up and to give up one key of the safe, while the other was obtained from one of the clerks.

In the meantime Dan Kelly had entered the private apartments attached to the bank by the back door, and was keeping guard to ensure that no one should leave the house. All the prisoners were searched for arms. Mr Scott was told that he must summon his wife and family and servants, and when he had done this, they, with the two clerks, were all put in the passage, under the eye of Dan Kelly and the muzzles of his revolvers. Ned Kelly, going out to the hawker's cart, brought from it a gunny bag, into which he shovelled all the money found in the teller's drawers, and the safe, mixing notes, gold, and silver pell-mell together. The total amount secured amounted to nearly £2,000 — £1,500 in notes and the balance in sovereigns and silver, in addition to which there were thirty ounces of gold dust. Kelly was very much disappointed at the smallness of his plunder, and told Scott he had expected to find at least £10,000 in the bank.

At first he threatened to carry away or burn the bank books, bills, securities, &c., but Scott persuaded him that this would do him no good, and finally he consented to leave them alone. The Scott household, in addition to the manager and other officers, consisted of Mrs Scott, seven children, and two servants who were all in the power of the bushrangers, and wondering what was to be done with them. They suffered no violence or indignity of any kind, but were told by Ned Kelly that they must get ready immediately for a drive to Faithfull's Creek. Mrs Scott seems to have been in no way alarmed by her meeting with the bushrangers, but, on the contrary, to have almost enjoyed the excitement of it, and she even chaffed Ned Kelly about his personal appearance, telling him that he was much more handsome and well-dressed man than she had expected, and by no means the ferocious ruffian she imaged him to be. These compliments evidently had a soothing effect on Ned Kelly's temper.

He told Mr Scott to put the horse into his (Mr Scott's) buggy, as, in addition to the outlaws' conveyances, it would be wanted to accommodate the large household from the bank. Mr Scott refused, saying his groom was out, and telling Kelly if he wanted the trap, to harness the horse himself. This was not at all the kind of language to which Kelly was accustomed from his prisoners, but Mrs Scott's flattery had induced a forgiving spirit in him, and accordingly he graciously consented to be his own groom.

The outlaws and the banker took a glass of whiskey together, Kelly, as precautionary measure, making Mr Scott drink first, and very soon afterwards a start was made for Faithfull's Creek. Hart rode as before; Kelly with Mr Scott and the plunder in the hawker's cart brought up the rear. Mrs Scott in front of him drove her husband's buggy and some of the children, and Dan Kelly, with Casement's cart and more of the household, led the way. A short distance from Euroa the funeral party before mentioned was met returning from the cemetery, and the bushrangers, getting their revolvers ready, gave an emphatic warning to their prisoners against attempting to make any sign. They were most obedient. None of the funeralists appeared to notice the vehicles or their passengers, and they soon passed one another. On the way to the station Ned Kelly talked freely to Mr Scott. He told him something of the police murders, showed him Kennedy's watch, and told him in a friendly way that he had narrowly escaped by being shot by Steve Hart for want of promptitude in putting up his hands and disrespect to himself, Ned Kelly, when the outlaws first entered the office. During the journey one of the horses in Kelly's vehicle fell, and a halt was made while the outlaws got out to put the horse on his feet and see to the harness, but without any other incident Faithfull's Creek was reached before dark.

Here the leader of the gang found everything just as he had left it, with the exception that the mob of prisoners had been added to by the capture of the telegraph repairer, Watt. Ned Kelly questioned him closely as to his movements and the time it would take to repair the break in the telegraph line, and then, having allowed the women and children to go into the kitchen, he shut up Scott and the clerks in the store.

After this, preparations were made in a leisurely way for departure. The horses were got in from the paddock, and the bag containing the plunder was strapped in front of Ned Kelly's saddle. In addition to the money five revolvers had been taken from the bank, and these, with Gloster's pistol and the rifle and guns of the shooting party, formed a considerable addition to the Kellys' armoury. The outlaws determined to have tea before they left, and they also amused themselves by giving exhibitions of their horsemanship of which they were very proud, allowing the men to stand outside the lock-up under guard to witness these feats. Ned Kelly in particular is reported to have distinguished himself as a horseman, galloping about, lying or sitting upon his saddle in all kinds of apparently impossible positions. Some of the men on patrol duty seem to have wandered a considerable distance from the house, and in so Hart must have encountered Mr Wyatt, who, it will be remembered, had been accosted most uncivilly by some stranger when he drove out from Euroa to view the broken lines. At any rate Mr McCauley reported afterwards that Steve Hart had asked him "who the old duffer was" whom he met on the road. The description given, and the fact that this was the day for Mr Wyatt's Licensing Court in Euroa, led Mr McCauley to say that it must have been the police magistrate. "By God," replied Hart;

"If I'd know that at the time, I would have popped him." Later in the day Mr Wyatt had another chance of being "popped", but nothing came of it. The train upon the engine of which he rode, and which stopped in front of Faithfull's Creek to allow him to examine the wires, naturally caused the outlaws some apprehension. Ned Kelly called out to the others that a trainload of bobbies had come to arrest them, and speaking in a tone of bravado for the prisoners' benefit, added that it did not matter, as they would shoot the whole —— lot of them. However, it proved to be a false alarm, and in a few minutes the train passed on without anybody from it approaching the homestead.

The Kellys by no means hurried themselves. Their meal and their riding exhibition took some time, and more they spent in conversing with the prisoners. It was evident that they wished to make a good impression, and to that end they showed great consideration to the women and made the servants gifts of money. To the boy who accompanied them to Euroa Ned Kelly also gave two pounds and the watch which he had taken from the body of Lonigan. The watch was afterwards handed over to the police. Apparently to make up for his loss, Ned Kelly asked Mr McDougall for his watch, but, on being told that it was a keepsake from M. McDougall's mother, magnanimously handed it back, robbing Mr McCauley instead, while Byrne appropriated Mr Scott's time-piece.

One of the outlaws' acts before leaving the station was to order some prisoners to burn the old clothes in exchange for which those of Gloster's cart had been taken, and this was done under Kelly's supervision. There was afterwards found, half-burnt, at the homestead, portion of a woman's hat, supposed to have been in one of the outlaw's swag, and this gave rise to the theory that Hart, who was young and slight, had carried a feminine disguise with him and sometimes worn it when travelling. Rumours had been current of a woman, supposed then to be Kate Kelly, being seen with the outlaws riding through the bush, and this gave colour to the belief that Hart sometimes masqueraded in female attire. At any rate, up to the day of the raid upon the station, no one had identified Hart as a member of the gang, and though Steele and others suspected him, it is said that only a few days before the robbery he was seen drinking at the bar of an hotel in Euroa and allowed to depart without question.

It was nearly nine o-clock and quite dark before the Kellys actually took their departure. Ned spoke a few last words to the prisoners, telling they were not to stir from the place for three hours. If they did he promised to track them down and shoot them wherever they might conceal themselves, and Mr McCauley in particular he was kind enough to make responsible for the good behaviour of the rest. The theatrical return for the alleged keepsake to Mr McDougall and the theft of the other watches were among the last acts of the outlaws before bidding their prisoners goodbye, after which, Dan Kelly and Steve Hart indulging in a little parting brag as to what they should do when they encountered the police, they rode away in the direction of the Strathbogie Ranges.

The prisoners, left to themselves, discussed what they should do, and there was a great preponderance of opinion in favour of remaining at the station for the time specified by Ned Kelly, or somewhere near it. None of them were so enthusiastic about giving early information as to run the risk of getting a bullet through their heads, should the outlaws have concealed themselves near the homestead, and apart from this chance it was suspected that sympathisers were near who would report their doings to the Kellys and perhaps cause them to be murdered later on when opportunity should offer. There were certainly no heroes among those stuck up at Faithfull's Creek as was abundantly shown by their action, or inaction, both before and after the bushrangers departed; but possibly the prisoners showed no more regard for their lives than would the majority of men. At any rate for some hours they waited patiently at the station, some of them whiling away the time by playing cards. About half-past ten or eleven, however, they thought it safe to leave their place of confinement, and while some of them went away to Euroa or elsewhere, others remained for the night at Faithfull's Creek. Before midnight the news of the robbery had been wired to Captain Standish on the information of those who ventured into the township, and in the early morning the police train from Benalla stopped at the station and gained the news of it there.

By this time the Kellys were far away—as far, at least, as they were anxious to go, which may have been after all but a few miles. At many places in the Strathbogie Ranges they had hiding places more or less secure, and there was afterwards reason to believe that for nearly a week they had been quietly camped at a bush hut not more than six miles distant from Euroa, waiting a favourable opportunity to make their raid upon the bank. Probably, not till the last minute had they decided what township to favour, as Mrs Skillion, the other sister, Kate Kelly, and one or two more of their relatives appear to have taken up their abode at different places from each one of which would have been accessible some haunt in the ranges. The one chosen by the outlaws was to depend on what town in the North-Eastern District they might bolt from, with the plunder of some bank in their possession.

12
A CHANGE IN THE COMMAND

A CURIOUS fatality seems to have attended upon all the police operations in connection with the Kelly outbreak at Euroa. Through someone's error the bank was left unprotected; even the one constable on duty was absent from the township when the bank was robbed; the departure of Mr Nicolson and Mr Sadlier for Albury took place at the most inopportune moment possible. Mr Wyatt's well-meant effort to detain them failed through mistakes incident to the hurry and confusion, together with the reticence of the train officials, and finally unexpected delay took place in the pursuit. Mr Wyatt doubtless acted wisely in stopping the train at Faithfull's Creek to learn particulars from Mr McCauley, and at Euroa itself more time was perhaps unavoidable wasted. No officer above the rank of senior constable had accompanied the special train from Benalla, and Mr Wyatt, from his own observation and remarks made to him by Senior Constable Johnson, and Detective Ward, saw good reason to suppose that there was likely to be a dispute as to the command between them. Ward asked him whether he thought it would be wise to start immediately upon the chase or to await the arrival of Mr Nicolson and Mr Sadlier, who had been wired to Albury to return as soon as possible; and, considering the jealousy often arising between the men of the detective service and the ordinary police, Mr Wyatt gave a guarded opinion in favour of waiting for the superior officers.

If they were likely to arrive within a few hours, he considered the value of their presence would more than compensate for any time lost. "I must put it thus," he said. "If it will delay you only a few hours, say two, or perhaps only three, I think you would be wise to stay for these reasons, viz., three of those men (the outlaws) are upon grass-fed horses and only one of them is shod. On the other hand your horses are all corn-fed, and in fine stable condition, and they are all shod; and in a twelve or twenty-four hours' pursuit, I do not think it signifies much, if you get well on the tracks, if you are two or three hours behind, compared with having your superior officer with you."

The men, falling in with this view, went out immediately to Faithfull's Creek station to pick up the outlaw's tracks and await the arrival of Mr Nicolson, while Mr Wyatt went by train to Benalla to meet the police officer there and acquaint him with all the news in his possession.

After leaving Benalla Mr Nicolson and Mr Sadlier had thought over the broken wires, and while not believing that the Kellys were responsible, they also deemed it possible that the outlaws or their associates had broken them to stop news coming down as they rode north to the Murray. In that case, by going to the Murray and watching the crossings, the police might intercept them, whereas in any case nothing could have been done towards following tracks from the broken wires during the night. On a small station up the line Mr Sadlier saw a man whom he knew to be one of the Kelly sympathisers, whose manner, which was apparently excited, caused a little uneasiness in Mr Sadlier's mind, suggesting that something was afoot, but he thought no more of the matter till, at Albury, Mr Nicolson received Captain Standish's telegram sent via Deniliquin, informing him of the Euroa robbery. Thereupon, with Mr Sadlier, he crossed the river to Wodonga in a spring cart and returned by the same train in which he had come. At Wangaratta a stop was made, and Mr Nicolson went to the hospital with the object of getting the black tracker who had been with him on the Murray on his former search, and who was a patient in the hospital. He was, however, too sick to leave, and Mr Nicolson was compelled to go without him, while on the morning of December 11 Mr Sadlier left the train, got together a police party, and searched for any tracks the Kellys might have made on their way from Euroa to some of their old haunts. They did find a track quite fresh, but after going some thirty of forty yards, the trackers, apparently, as on the former occasion, afraid for their lives, declared that they could follow it no further. Mr Sadlier went ahead into the scrub beyond where the tracks had been dropped in case there should be some ambush there, but found nothing. The purpose was to get to a farmhouse near Lake Rowan in the neighbourhood of Glenrowan, the residence of a friend of the Kellys and to watch it all night, but it was impossible to make the tracker work; consequently the house was not found and searched till next day when no trace of anything was discovered.

Meanwhile Mr Nicolson had gone on to Benalla where he arrived in the early morning, telegraphed to the police at Mansfield asking for two trackers, and then went on with Mr Wyatt, who was waiting for him, to Faithfull's Creek.

Stopping the train there at about 8.30, he got out and met the party of police who had ridden out from Euroa, while Mr Wyatt continued his journey.

At Faithfull's Creek there was a good deal of confusion. Sympathisers or busybodies, under pretence of seeking for the tracks of the outlaws, had galloped about all round the place, making it very difficult to pick them up.

One of the overseers gave Mr Nicolson some trouble and caused delay, but eventually following the directions of the housekeeper, by whose common sense he was impressed, Mr Nicolson took his men in the direction—towards Euroa—in which she said she had last seen the dust of the outlaws' horses. There tracks were picked up and followed, the troublesome overseer presently getting a fall from his horse and dropping out of the party, much to Mr Nicolson's satisfaction. By midday the police were in Euroa, most of them absolutely knocked up. The majority had only just returned from a search party with Mr Nicolson before the robbery, and he felt it necessary to allow them some rest and refreshment. For this he was blamed in some quarters for procrastination, but he emphatically denies that there was anything of the kind, and declares that the men were so overcome with heat and fatigue that they actually dropped asleep over their food before they had eaten or drunk anything provided for them. Johnson, one of the most energetic men of the party, slept so heavily, that the hotelkeeper, believing he had sunstroke, poured water over him, but even this failed to wake him. In that state Mr Nicolson could do nothing with his troopers so he ordered a halt until six o'clock, during which time the men slept, and after a meal he led them away towards Murchison, a township lying near due north, in which direction, from what he had learnt from people at Faithfull's Creek, Mr Nicolson thought it likely the outlaws would be making.

During that night nothing of them was heard or seen, and any trucks they might have left would be impossible to follow in the darkness. About six next morning the men returned to Euroa for rest, and Mr Nicolson lay down but could not sleep, as he was ill from continuous fatigue, and suffering in particular from his eyes, which were so inflamed as to make him almost blind.

Captain Standish arrived from Melbourne in the course of the morning. After discussion with Mr Nicolson he agreed to send a police party away that day into the Strathbogie Ranges; but as Mr Nicolson was absolutely broken down in health and unfit to accompany it the Commissioner telegraphed for Mr Hare to come up from Melbourne and take command.

Mr Hare arrived at Euroa that afternoon but he by no means felt inclined to start with the police party to the Strathbogie Ranges, for he knew nothing of the circumstances, and he told Captain Standish that, for this reason and because he felt very unwell, it would be most unfair to send him out. Captain Standish, who was always ready to attach great weight—too great weight it was generally supposed in the service—to the opinions and wishes of Mr Hare, very readily fell in with this view, and the police party departed under the leadership of Senior- Constable Johnson. They remained away for six or seven days in the bush without discovering anything, and on their return reported themselves at Benalla.

From this day there began a new regime in the Kelly pursuit, Mr Nicolson going to Melbourne to take the Chief Commissioner's place in charge of general and office work, while Captain Standish made Benalla his head- quarters and directed operations against the outlaws with the assistance of Mr Hare.

By these officers the system of rushing police all over the country in search parties, which Mr Nicolson had followed, more and more against his own judgement, was vigorously pursued. Just before the Euroa robbery, Mr Nicolson, as private letters of his witnessed, had decided, had he remained in command, to follow a new plan, endeavouring to secure more accurate knowledge and better espionage of the Kellys by agents, and never sending police parties after them except upon the most definite and reliable information. The vague search, he had found, broke down the strength of troopers and horses and made the police more or less a laughing-stock to the people of the district, who knew that every move was watched and reported by active Kelly sympathisers, who would be galloping away into the bush, with news almost before the police party had left the barracks.

Mr Wyatt disapproved of this system; Mr Sadlier described it as "fooling," and Superintendent Nicolson, though against his better judgement he had adopted it and kept the police uselessly active in order to satisfy the public opinion in the colony, had come to recognise the futility of such measures.

Nevertheless, Captain Standish, or rather Mr Hare, who had great influence over the Commissioner, pinned his faith to the police-galloping system. In other cases it had had great effect. Ben Hall and Morgan, two notorious bushrangers of earlier dates in New South Wales and Victoria, had been kept constantly on the move, never getting a moment's rest until Morgan was reported to have said that he would rather be dead than live the miserable hunted life that was his, and finally he was shot at Peechelba, near the border of Victoria and New South Wales. But to hunt and harass the Kellys, as these solitary men were hunted, was a far more difficult task, owing to the numerous sources of information, concealment and supply that number of their relatives and sympathisers afforded them. Of blood relations of the Kellys there were said to be seventy- seven in the district, while the number of their connections and loyal sympathisers was legion. Doubtless the Euroa bank robbery did much to add to the ranks of their friends and to increase the loyalty and admiration of existing ones, for the outlaws, having no chance for personally spending the money, largely used it for distribution among their relatives and agents who purchased them ammunition and supplies. Kate Kelly and Mrs Skillion were observed to launch out into great extravagance in dress and to have their pockets full of money immediately after the robbery.

In one respect Captain Standish and Mr Hare were in a better position for vigorous action than Mr Nicolson, since, after the Euroa robbery, not only was the strength of the police increased but a number of the garrison artillery were sent to townships in the district to secure their safety from raiding, thus setting still more of the police free for active patrol work.

The expense incurred by the country on account of the Kelly outbreak had already been considerable. From October 26 to December 12 it amounted to £3,408, of which the largest items were £1,000 odd for arms, ammunition and equipment, and £1,000 for travelling allowances to the police, the later expense arising from the fact that men were merely temporarily transferred for duty in the Kelly district, and during their presence there for months at a time received a 5s. per day allowance in excess of their ordinary pay.

The Euroa robbery threw the whole colony of Victoria into a wonderful state of indignation and alarm. The Government increased the reward for the apprehension of the Kellys from £500 to £1,000 per head. The banks in large and populous towns, hundreds of miles from the Kelly country, strengthened their premises against attack and armed the bank officials with revolvers. The outlaws were the constant subject of conversation in every corner of the country. "Police and Kellys" became a favourite game among school children everywhere in Victoria, and a game in which the Kellys were always victorious.

Then and for many months afterwards the policeman's lot was not a happy one, if contempt and abuse, very largely undeserved, were calculated to make him unhappy. All the mistakes made by the police were exaggerated, and the most absurd tales were told of their deliberate wish to avoid the outlaws and their refusal to venture into places where they knew them to be. Irresponsible writers, who understood none of the tremendous difficulties which the nature of the country and the people put in the way of pursuit, spoke glibly of the disgrace incurred by the police in not capturing the outlaws off-hand, and assured the public that had they control of affairs things would go very differently. It cannot be doubted that mistakes were made. There was a want of concert between the police and the other Government departments, as was shown by the fact that no information was given to the police of the breakage of the telegraph lines at Faithfull's Creek, whereas an early report might have changed everything. But where the police were to blame the fault seems, as a rule, to have lain at headquarters rather than with the officers actively engaged. The latter, with very few exceptions, worked pluckily, intelligently, and hard; but Captain Standish showed a certain lack of enthusiasm and energy in the supreme direction of affairs which was most discouraging to those under him, while his evident partiality for Mr Hare and his inclination almost to thwart Mr Nicolson were productive of anything but good feeling and discipline in the force. Mr Hare unfortunately, more especially at a later date than up to the time of the Euroa robbery, did more to aggravate than to smooth away the jealousies occasioned by Captain Standish's ill-advised conduct. Active, energetic, courageous and popular with his men, Mr Hare was too little inclined to credit his brother officers with the possession of the same qualities; and his egotism, which led him to take an undue share of credit to himself for every good move, was both during and after the Kelly operations a legitimate cause of soreness and bitterness to the other leaders of the police associated with him. He, however, entered upon his new duties in the North-Eastern District with the utmost confidence and enthusiasm, and great things were expected of his association with Captain Standish, in the way of a speedy termination to the Kelly gang's career.

13
THE KELLY GANG AT JERILDERIE

AFTER Captain Standish and Mr Hare had made arrangements for distributing the garrison artillery in squads of six or seven through the disaffected district, and had added to the police strength in many townships, Mr Hare gave his attention to more active work. Rumours, most of them absolutely baseless, were arriving every day concerning appearances by the outlaws, or some of them, at places in all corners of the district and out of it. A squatter sent word post-haste to Benalla that the outlaws were shooting parrots near his garden, and this with many other statements just as absurd received enquiry from the police and kept the men employed. Mr Hare, however, for some weeks, accompanied no search parties himself, his time being fully taken up in making himself acquainted with the police under his command and the private agents in Government employ. This work for a long time kept him travelling from station to station over thousands of square miles of rough, hilly country. On his recommendation some of the smartest men were promoted to the rank of senior constable, in order to give them authority to command the search parties which were everywhere organised for the use when they should be wanted.

From December 12 to the end of the year nothing of any moment took place; but at the beginning of 1879 Captain Standish, Mr Hare and Mr Sadlier in consultation together, and with the approval of the Government, determined to put the outlawry Act in operation against a number of known or suspected Kelly sympathisers. The greatest secrecy was preserved with regard to this intention. Had it become known that arrests were to be made there might have been as much trouble in catching the sympathisers as in catching their principals; and accordingly, after a black list had been made on information supplied by Detective Ward and several of the police, about twenty men, resident in different parts of the Kelly country, were all arrested on one day and lodged in the Beechworth gaol.

The value of this move at this particular time was, to say the least of it, extremely doubtful. No doubt it to some extent embarrassed the outlaws by depriving them of the services of many of their agents and diminishing their sources of food and other supplies, but at the same time it roused a bitterly hostile feeling against the police in the minds even of many who had no sympathy with the Kellys. Had there been available evidence upon which to commit the accused for trial the matter would have been different, but in nearly all the cases, though everyone felt morally certain that the prisoners were well disposed to the Kellys and were ready to help them, if they had not done so, there was no overt act in contravention of the law that could be proved against them. The result was that when the cases came on for hearing a police officer appeared at Beechworth and applied for a week's remand, which was granted by the police magistrate. When the court sat again a remand was again asked for, on the grounds that to call the evidence of private people at that time would put their lives in danger from the outlaws, and that to call the police would necessitate taking them away from urgent duty. These excuses were flimsy. Counsel for the prisoners protested bitterly against this infraction of British justice involved in the continued imprisonment of persons against whom no charges supported by evidence were disclosed, but the police 'magistrate, with a hint from the Government, declared that exceptional cases demanded exceptional measures, and granted the remand. So from week to week the farce continued, the public growing more incensed, the prisoners more insulting and defiant, and the police officers themselves more disgusted with the false position in which they were placed, and the waste of time, caused by going every week to Beechworth on their unpopular task of asking for further illegal imprisonment of the sympathisers.

However, they remained in gaol, and had a larger number been so arbitrarily treated results of some kind might have followed; but many of the Kellys' best friends were still at large, including their sisters and other female relatives, while injustice was winning over others from the side of the law to theirs.

In the beginning of February, when the Beechworth gaol was still full of sympathisers, Aaron Sherritt, the agent engaged by Mr Sadlier early in the pursuit, came to Mr Hare in Benalla with important news. Mr Hare was greatly impressed by the men's personality and honesty of purpose, and flattered himself that his feelings were reciprocated. Describing their interview later, he wrote: "Somehow or other, I made a most wonderful impression on him. I had some drink with him, and saw that my influence over him was very great."

Whether Sherritt was as greatly impressed as Mr Hare believed or not, he communicated important news to the effect that on the previous afternoon at his hut, which lay among the hills near Beechworth, midway between the elder Sherritt's and Mrs Byrne's, he had met Joe Byrne and Dan Kelly. Dan, he said, had been suspicious and kept at a distance; but Joe Byrne had jumped off his horse and entered into a long conversation, during which he had asked Sherritt to join the gang and accompany them to Goulburn, a town in New South Wales, where the Kellys had relatives and which they proposed to visit. Sherritt refused, whereupon Byrne admitted he was right not to mix himself up with them and get into trouble, and rode away with Dan Kelly. Sherritt noted the brands of their horses which he gave to Mr Hare, and told him that one outlaw rode a bay and the other a grey, both very fine animals. Giving Sherritt two pounds for his information and advising him not to let himself be seen in Benalla, Mr Hare immediately sent warning telegrams to the Victorian police on the border and to the police of New South Wales. News shortly arrived that on the evening of the day named by Sherritt men supposed to be Byrne and Dan Kelly had been seen riding towards the Murray, and a police party was sent up the river to watch a crossing place where a chain of hills on either side of the river runs all the way to Goulburn.

Nothing was heard or seen of the bushrangers till some five or six days later, when on the evening of February 10 a telegram arrived informing Captain Standish that they had been at Jerilderie, a town in New South Wales some sixty miles beyond the Victorian border. On this information police parties were immediately despatched to watch every crossing place in the hope of intercepting the Kellys on their return from New South Wales.

By this time all Australia was astonished by the news of an exploit more audacious in some respects than any the bushrangers had perpetrated before.

Leaving Victoria on the day they talked with Sherritt, they probably met beyond the border; at any rate all four of them, riding quietly together, took their way, not towards Goulburn, but to Jerilderie, a township containing three or four hundred inhabitants, distant about sixty miles from the Murray.

The country in its vicinity is not rough and mountainous like the bushrangers' native haunts, but a dead level plain, dotted sparsely here and there with clumps of timber. The outlaws, however, crossed over it unobserved, and late on the night on Saturday, March 8, they called at the police station which lies at some little distance from the township. The two constables, Richards and Devine, and the wife and family of Devine, who occupied the station, had all gone to bed. They were awakened by a loud knocking at the door and a call to the police to get up as a drunken man in the township had committed a murder at Davidson's Hotel. Both constables, going to the door undressed and unarmed, listened for some time to the details of an imaginary disturbance which Ned Kelly poured into their ears while he waited to see if any other constables would come out of the barracks. Satisfied presently that there were no more police to deal with, the outlaws suddenly produced loaded revolvers and bailed up the two constables, who, seeing nothing but death before them if they resisted, gave in with the best grace they could. Entering the barracks and closing the door, the Kellys placed Devine and Richards in their own lock-up for the night. Mrs Divine, in her night-dress, was made to show the outlaws over the premises in case other men might be concealed there, and after Ned Kelly had secured all the arms in the barracks she was, with her children, allowed to go to rest. Steve Hart was left in the house as sentry, and he let Mrs Devine know that on any attempt to escape she and the imprisoned constables would be immediately shot. In the meantime the other bushrangers made their horses comfortable in the police stables, after which they went into the police station to take up their quarters for the night.

When morning came Ned Kelly and Joe Byrne dressed themselves in the constables' uniforms and moved about the yard and barracks in sight of anyone who might be passing, without attracting any attention. From Mrs. Devine they learnt that she was accustomed to sweep and get ready the court- house in which a Roman Catholic Church service was held, and to avoid exciting suspicion she was allowed to do so as usual, Joe Byrne in uniform accompanying her and escorting her back to the station. In the afternoon Hart and Byrne, both dressed as constables, took Richards out of the lock-up and made him accompany them in a walk through the town, that they might learn the run of the streets and the position of the buildings. Richards was warned that if anyone accosted the party, under penalty of being immediately shot through the head, he was to introduce the bushrangers as new constables just sent up to Jerilderie to give the town extra protection against the Kelly gang. On their return to the police station Richards was reincarcerated, and the bushrangers, making Mrs. Devine prepare their meals, spent the remainder of the afternoon and the night undisturbed.

On Monday morning Joe Byrne, in uniform, took two of the horses to be shod by the police farrier, who did the work but apparently was rendered somewhat suspicious by Byrne's manner, for he was careful to note the brands of the horses.

About eleven o'clock Ned and Dan Kelly, wearing police costume, took Richards with them into the town, while Byrne and Hart followed in their own clothes on horseback. Their first move was to take possession of the Royal Hotel, adjoining the Bank of New South Wales which they intended to rob. Mr Cox, the proprietor, was introduced by Richards to Ned Kelly, who told him he must give up to the gang some rooms in the hotel for the reception of anyone he might take prisoner. Mr Cox, who showed Kelly over the place, was confined himself in the big dining-room as a beginning, and the other three bushrangers, taking up positions in the bar and elsewhere, marched off the servants and everyone who came near the hotel to the dining-room. When a mob of prisoners had been secured the bushrangers turned their attention to the bank. Mr Living, the accountant, hearing someone at the back door, went to tell him that he must not enter there, and found himself confronted by Joe Byrne with a revolver in his hand. To an inquiry who he was Byrne answered, "the Kelly gang," and ordered Living to give up all firearms in the bank. Mr Mackin, another clerk who had been standing in the street, on hearing the noise entered the bank, and was ordered by Joe Byrne to jump over the counter and join himself and Living. Since Byrne was pointing two revolvers at him, Mackin promptly obeyed.

He and Living allowed themselves to be conducted to the hotel next door and were confronted by Ned Kelly, who asked them where Mr Jarleton, the manager and only remaining official of the bank, was to be found. The clerks said he had just returned from a journey and was in his dressing room, whereupon Ned Kelly and Byrne went back to the bank but failed to find him. Ned therefore called Living away from the hotel and told him he must find Mr Jarleton promptly. As it turned out, he was in his bath preparatory to dressing himself after a long dusty ride. Living told him the bank was stuck up and that he must dress as quickly as possible and surrender himself, which Mr Jarleton was forced to do, Dan Kelly coming over from the hotel to take charge of him.

In the meantime Ned Kelly and Byrne were engaged in appropriating all the money in the bank, making Living show them where it was to be found. When some £700, the teller's cash, had been taken, Mr Elliot, the local schoolmaster, entered the bank and was told by Kelly to jump over the counter. He professed himself unable to do so, but the sight of Ned Kelly's revolver muzzle gave him unwonted activity, and after all he found it possible. Kelly, who again expected to get £10,000, was unsatisfied with the teller's cash and demanded more from Living, who told some plucky though useless falsehoods, saying that nothing of any value was in the safe, but Kelly refused to believe him and brought in the manager, getting from him the duplicate key. The other he had already obtained from Living. From the safe £1,450 was taken, and also a number of bank books, which, in spite of remonstrances, Kelly burnt, probably being under the impression that he was thereby doing a good turn for poor debtors of the bank.

While the outlaws were in the office Mr Rankin and Mr Gill, two townsmen, entered and were told to bail up, but instead of obeying they made a bolt into the street. Rankin was caught and very roughly handled by Kelly who took him into the hotel, and making him stand apart from the others against a wall in the passage, said he would shoot him. Rankin, who was a well-known merchant and a justice of the peace, behaved most pluckily in these trying circumstances, and all the other prisoners begged Kelly not to fire. He made a great show of unwillingness to be merciful, one would suppose in order to inspire salutary fear, for even his spirit of domineering vanity could scarcely induce him to commit murder for such trifling cause as a momentary refusal to obey him. Whatever his real intentions may have been, the prisoners spent a most uncomfortable time, for Dan Kelly and Hart were quite anxious to fire into them for the offence of interceding for Rankin, and Ned Kelly declared that before he left he was going to shoot Richards and Devine. In fact he said his object in coming to the town had been simply to kill them, and that the robbing of the bank was a mere incident in his visit.

After dealing with Mr Rankin, Ned Kelly, accompanied by Living and Richards, went in search of Mr Gill, the other man who had fled from the bank, but he had hidden himself away in the bed of a creek and they were unable to find him. This was a great disappointment to Kelly as Mr Gill was the editor of the local newspaper, and the bushranger wished him to print an account of his life and great deeds, which he had either written himself or got some friend—perhaps Joe Byrne who was the litterateur of the gang—to write for him.

Not being able to see the editor, Kelly called at his house where he met Mrs Gill and endeavoured to persuade her to take the manuscript, saying he would pay for the printing; but she steadily refused to have anything to do with the matter, and, to prevent Kelly's temper becoming more dangerous, Living asked for the writing, promising that he would see that it was printed. Mr Living kept his word; and the production—a bombastic eulogy of Kelly's prowess, with tirades against the police and some account of the murders at the Wombat—eventually appeared in print

For some hours after the bank had been robbed the outlaws held possession of the town, and though acting in some respects with apparent rashness, they really made their safety secure by the number of hostages they had all the time under the revolver muzzles of one or more of them. Ned Kelly walked about the town and entered another hotel where there were several people, any of whom he said might kill him, but with the result of the wholesale slaughter in the township.

At Jerilderie it was particularly noticeable that Ned Kelly and Byrne were the leading spirits of the gang — Ned in undisputed authority, but Byrne an able and trusted lieutenant, while the other two played minor parts and were treated by Ned Kelly in the most contemptuous fashion. Between him and Hart there was some temper shown, and it appeared on one occasion that revolvers might be used. Hart had stolen watches and other property from several of the prisoners who complained to Kelly. The leader was most indignant, called Hart a "thing," and made him return the stolen property. One of Hart's prizes was taken from a Wesleyan clergyman and, in ordering Hart to give it back, Kelly told him if he wanted a watch to get a good one. Acting on this principle himself, he robbed the bank manager.

While Kelly was engaged in search for a publisher, Joe Byrne had taken command of the telegraph office. He bailed up the operator and ordered men to sever the wires and cut down eight posts, after which he amused himself by overhauling all the messages which had gone through the telegraph office that day, and when Kelly arrived the two broke a number of insulators with their revolvers. Mr Jefferson, the telegraph master, was told that if he repaired the line before next day he would be visited later on and shot by the gang.

After Ned Kelly had taken a blood mare from the stables of Mr McDougall, an hotel-keeper, and the outlaws had completed their business in the town, the leader made a speech to the prisoners, trying to appeal to their sympathies by an account of his wrongs and a garbled account of the Wombat murders, also telling them that the next move of the gang would be to rob the bank of Urana, another New South Wales town.

He then took Constable Richards back to the police station and locked him up, after which he returned to the hotel and gave the prisoners leave to depart, first "shouting" a number of them to drinks in the bar. Before this, towards evening, he had sent Byrne away leading a pack horse, with the money in a bag strapped to the saddle. He himself was next to leave, and led with him one of the police horses. Dan Kelly and Steve Hart departed last, and, before they took leave of the town they galloped up and down the streets, flourishing revolvers and singing songs in praise of their gang. It was well for the townspeople that no mischief happened to them after Ned Kelly and Byrne had gone, for the other two scoundrels seemed to take pleasure in cruelty for its own sake, and had shown a most unpleasant anxiety to shoot someone or other all through the day. It time, however, they too relieved the town of their presence and the inhabitants were able to breathe freely. It is to the credit of the telegraph master, Mr Jefferson, that undeterred by the Kellys' threats he immediately set to work to repair the line, and by nine o'clock that night Mr Hare in Benalla received a wire telling him of the robbery at Jerilderie.

14
THE CAMP AT MRS. BYRNE'S

POLICE parties sent out with all possible despatch on receipt of the news from Jerilderie watched every crossing-place on the Murray, but without the least effect. Probably they arrived at the river too late, but at any rate it was soon commonly known that the Kellys were at home again in the Strathbogie Ranges, or some other part of the mountainous North-Eastern District. They may have ridden back together, for they were reported to have met at a station twenty miles from Jerilderie, or they may have separated and come together again at some Victorian rendezvous.

One result of the exploit was an increase of the reward offered by the Government for the capture of the outlaws to £1,000 per head, and an offer of the same amount by the New South Wales Government and banks, so that the destruction of the gang became worth £8,0000 to any man who could accomplish it. Blood money, however, owing either to fear of the outlaws, or to some worthier instinct, had no apparent attraction for men who knew the Kellys' whereabouts. There were numbers of perfectly law-abiding residents who at various times could have told the exact position of the Kelly camps, but they did not choose to do so. Just after the Jerilderie affair Ned Kelly, disguised and muffled up, was recognised by a farmer on the King River some forty miles from Benalla at whose house he called, and others were aware that the outlaws had a camp close by, but they made no mention of these things. They had no sympathy with crime. On the whole they would have been glad to see the Kellys caught, but an abstract respect for the law was not sufficient to make them run risks of having their lives taken, or their stacks and fences burnt and their cattle killed or driven away. The Kellys, they knew, would not harm them. Except in murdering Kennedy, the outlaws had done nothing which particularly shocked the average bush farmer's conscience, and even with regard to the police murders Kelly had succeeded to some extent in fostering a belief that the constables were killed in fair fight. The bank robberies were not altogether displeasing to poor farmers rather inclined to regard banks as their enemies and fair game for anyone smart enough to get the better of them. Accordingly, while they were left alone—and the Kellys, having soared above such small annoying tricks as stealing their neighbours' stock, were unlikely to harm them—a large number of people who saw and heard of the outlaws frequently decided to let the police catch them as best they might without taking any part in the game.

On the Saturday after the robbery, Mr. Hare, whose faith in Sherritt's bona fides was strengthened by late events, went to see him at Beechworth, and learnt that on previous Wednesday Dan Kelly had been at Mrs. Byrne's and had breakfasted there. The gang, he said, had separated after leaving Jerilderie and were to meet at a certain place; but the others had not kept their appointment, and he was in search of news of them. Sherritt believed that the whole gang would be at Mrs Byrne's on the following night and he asked Mr Hare to bring men to watch the place. Detective Ward, who was present at the conversation, distrusted Sherritt and told Mr Hare that though the man could put the outlaws into his power he did not believe that for all the money in the world he would betray his friend, Joe Byrne. Sherritt was at this time engaged to Byrne's sister, and for the credit of human nature one hopes that Ward was right; but Mr Hare thought otherwise, and the evidence is inconclusive, though there is little doubt that Sherritt cared far more for the reward money than for his faith towards other members of the gang.

Next night Mr Hare and Detective Ward met Sherritt at a place agreed on, where they were to have been joined by a party of police of the township of Eldorado, but by a mischance these men did not appear, and accordingly, pluckily determining to go alone, Mr Hare and Detective Ward trusted themselves to the guidance of Sherritt and set out on a pitch- black night for a ride through the rough, stony and scrubby mountains. After riding for some time Aaron Sherritt halted and pointed out a glimmer of firelight through the trees. It was the bushrangers, he said. This was their country into which no-one else ventured, and for once they had been careless enough to betray themselves by enjoying the comfort of a fire, instead of seeking safety by freezing in their camp on the coldest nights as they were usually reported to do. On instructions from Mr Hare, Sherritt got down from his horse and sneaked forward to make certain who the men by the fire might be, and in a few minutes he returned. "Where do you think the fire is, Mr Hare?" he asked.

"About 150 yards away," was the reply, to which Aaron answered that it was three miles or more. Mr Hare believed that Sherritt had sold him, but on riding forward found that he spoke the truth, for they reached the edge of a precipice and saw that the fire which had looked so near was on the other side of a deep gully, with the Woolshed diggings on the flat between.

Disappointed here, the party rode away to watch Mrs Byrne's house, which lay in the gully under the lee of a steep hill. Sherritt, crawling up to the window, listened for a time and returned, saying that the gang were not yet arrived, but he pointed out the spot where they were accustomed to tie their horses, and led the two officers to a hiding-place near a stockyard by which he advised waiting and watching all night, as through the stockyard the outlaws always passed on their way to the house. The police waited; the outlaws did not come, but Sherritt was confident that before long they would do so, and said that if the police wanted to get them they must watch the house.

Mr Hare determined to follow this advice. Riding back to Beechworth in the morning, he made arrangements for a permanent camp in the gully about a mile from the Byrnes' hut. To this camp he brought seven men, and placed four more in another, high above it in the mountains at a spot which commanded the gully below, and to which Sherritt said the Kellys often came. For twenty-five days and nights Mr. Hare and his men underwent severe hardships and ran considerable danger in their watch for the Kellys. During the day they rested, exposed to the heat of the sun and without any cover, while at night they crept down and watched Mrs Byrne's house till morning, returning half frozen at dawn to their comfortless camp. Fires were forbidden lest the smoke should give the outlaws warning, but all Mr Hare's precautions against discovery were in vain. The Kellys did not come, and after the twentieth day Mrs Byrne, who for some reason suspected police were about, discovered a piece of soap near the creek, and a stick which a constable had been whittling to amuse himself, while later on the reflection of the sun on a sardine tin on the hill-side caught her eye, and, going to investigate its meaning, she stumbled upon the police camp. Mr Hare's chief concern seems to have been for Sherritt, whose chance of life would have been small had he been seen with the police and remained afterwards in the district. Sherritt realised his danger and on Mr Hare's advice left the camp immediately at his best speed, in order to prove an alibi, by showing himself to other friends of the Kellys at a distance, returning to join the police in the evening.

After this discovery Mr Hare wished to break up the camp, but Sherritt assured him that Mrs Byrne had, except through him, no means of communicating with the outlaws, and that there was still hope of effecting a capture. Taking a penny whistle with him that evening he approached the Byrnes' house, on the way making music which he hoped would bring out his girl to meet him and enable him to learn just what Mrs Byrne knew. The Byrnes of course would suppose him to come from his own hut which was not far distant from theirs.

Miss Byrne did not go to meet Sherritt, but the old lady drew him aside and told him she had discovered the police, rating Aaron at the same time for his stupidity for not doing so. He expressed the utmost surprise and some incredulity, but his mind was relieved by feeling that he was not suspected, and on his persuasion Mr Hare remained in his camp for five more days.

During one of the night watches, at about ten o'clock, a man on foot passed close by Mr Hare and his men on the way to Mrs Byrne's house. Mr Hare did not challenge or fire, for Sherritt, he remembered, was at the Byrnes' and could bring word back as to who the stranger was. Accordingly, though he suspected him to be Joe Byrne, much to the astonishment of the constables Mr Hare allowed the man to walk through the midst of them. When Aaron returned from the Byrnes' about two hours later Mr Hare waited to see if he would make mention of any strangers having been at the house. He did not do so, and on being questioned upon the subject, said, yes, a man named Scotty who came from the hills had been there. Mr Hare was not satisfied. He believed the man to be Joe Byrne, for if there were any one of the gang whom Aaron might refuse to betray it would be he, and it seems somewhat extraordinary under the circumstances that nothing further was done. Mr. Hare makes no mention of the man's departure from the house, and apparently the police party returned to the camp, leaving to his own devices the stranger who Mr Hare then believed at least might be Joe Byrne, and whom later he still more strongly suspected.

There is much reason to doubt whether the existence of Mr Hare's camp was from the very beginning a secret to the outlaws or their friends, though its exact position may have been unknown. The police horses were put in Aaron Sherritt's paddock, where their presence was likely to be observed and to excite suspicion; and it appears that almost from the inception of the enterprise Mrs Byrne had observed policemen's tracks, which the sympathisers always recognised since the constables wore distinctive boots, while such carelessness as casually leaving about soap, whittled sticks, and sardine tin argues very badly for the intelligence with which the ambush was conducted.

Some five days after Mrs Byrne caught sight of the police Mr Hare came to the conclusion that it was useless to waste more time in the gully and left the camp, though his men were kept there for about a fortnight longer.

During the time Mr Hare was in the camp Sherritt spent his days as a rule at his own place or his mother's, which was near it, but he occasionally put in a few hours with the police, when he told the superintendent much of the ways of horse stealers generally and of himself and the Kellys in particular. For his own part he confessed that, even if he obtained the reward and fulfilled his ambition by purchasing a fine stallion and some good mares to breed first-class horses, he still would find more pleasure in stealing than in breeding them. One of the best dodges for altering brands, he explained, was to pull out the hair with a pair of tweezers to add or change a letter, and to paint over the depilated part with iodine, which made the skin appear as if it were branded in the ordinary way, and this process, he said, he and the Kellys had often executed with great success. For Ned Kelly's determination, resource, and powers of endurance he had an almost superstitious admiration. Mr Hare had expressed astonishment at his (Aaron's) ability to sleep upon the ground when the temperature was below freezing point, uncovered by any blanket and not wearing even a coat, and he asked if the outlaws possessed the same iron constitutions. According to Aaron, Ned Kelly had twice his physical powers in every way, but he considered himself a better man than any of the other three.

On March 6, when Mr Hare was watching for the Kellys at Mrs Byrnes', the forces engaged in hunting the outlaws were added to by the arrival from Queensland of a Queensland officer, Sub-Inspector O'Connor, a white senior constable, and six native black trackers—Corporal Sambo, and troopers Hero, Johnny, Jimmy, Barney, and Jack. Early in the Kelly campaign the Queensland authorities had offered the services of some of their native police, who did excellent work in the northern colony in following tracks often invisible to white men, but Captain Standish had been averse to employing them, though Mr Sadlier and Mr Nicolson made use when they could of Victorian aboriginals who possessed something of the same skill. However, after the Jerilderie affair Captain Standish saw the necessity of taking every possible measure against the Kellys, and sank his own prejudices against the trackers in so far as to allow of the acceptance of the men offered by Queensland. On their arrival he met them and their officer, Mr O'Connor, at Albury, and experiments were very shortly made of their powers of tracking. These, though carried out under conditions which by no means satisfied Mr O'Connor, greatly impressed the Victorian officers, including even Captain Standish, who nevertheless to the last maintained that they were comparatively useless in following men who moved in celerity which characterised the journeys of the Kellys. This, however, was not the opinion of Mr Hare, Mr Sadlier, and Mr Nicolson, who placed great reliance on the trackers, nor of the Kellys, who feared them more than all the other police in the district.

Very shortly after the black trackers' arrival one of the troopers died of congestion of the lungs, and all of them seemed to feel the change from the warm climate of Queensland to the frosty air of the Victorian highlands. For a time Mr O'Connor, Mr Sadlier, Captain Standish and Mr Hare all lived in unity together at police head-quarters in Benalla, but before Mr O'Connor had been very long in the colony unfortunate quarrels arose between him and Captain Standish, with the result that much of the usefulness of the trackers was discounted by Captain Standish's refusal to employ them on certain occasions when reliable news of the outlaws had been obtained.

To give a detailed account of the work done by Mr Hare during the months from December, 1878, to July, 1879, that he remained on duty in the North-Eastern District would be impossible without filling hundreds of pages.

During nearly the whole of that time he was constantly engaged in search parties, and on several occasions must have been very close upon the Kellys.

The fact was, however, that being close upon the outlaws many times gave the police no reasonable cause to suppose that they would once actually obtain touch with them; for, at least as well mounted as the police, the Kellys were man for man better horsemen and far more intimately acquainted with the country. Given one hundred yards' start of a constable, there was but the remotest chance of the outlaws being captured or hit. They could gallop through timber and down mountain-sides that more gently bred horsemen would hesitate about attempting at a walk, and once out of sight they might strike north, south, east or west, leaving no clue behind them which would be of the slightest use to the police if they hoped to make a rapid pursuit. With the assistance of the trackers it was no doubt possible to slowly and painfully follow the outlaws, keeping them constantly on the move; but there was really little chance of shooting or capturing them except by lying in wait for them and surprising them on a visit to their friends. This, however, was also extremely difficult, for information of the Kellys' intentions was only obtainable through spies, and with these the Kellys were better supplied than the police both as to numbers and good faith.

Sympathy secured the outlaws much assistance; money secured them much more, and it was clear that they spent money freely, for notes which were known by their numbers to have gone to the bank at Jerilderie were in circulation all through the North-Eastern District.

Mr Hare says himself that the police parties, though they did not wear uniform, were all "as well known as the town clock," and that agents of the Kellys hung about every police station and every railway station in the district, ready to gallop away at a moment's notice on the police making any move. No doubt the constant search caused some anxiety to the Kellys, but in spite of it they enjoyed a good deal of their friends' society.

They even, it seems, intended to go to a race meeting at a township named Whorouly, not far from Beechworth, and Aaron Sherritt received a letter from Joe Byrne, asking him to ride a horse of Byrne's at the meeting.

This letter Sherritt brought to Mr Hare, who sent police, disguised as three-card trick men, to the meeting. Mr Hare himself attended and was greatly amused by certain people pointing out Aaron Sherritt to him as a notorious Kelly sympathiser, and urging that he should be arrested for the theft of a very fine horse he was riding, since he could never have come by it honestly—the said horse having been purchased only a few days before by Mr Hare for Sherritt's use. Mr Hare pleaded ignorance of the man and his doings, and looked forward to the developments the day might bring forth; but Joe Byrne, who had arranged to meet Sherritt at the back of the course, must have been warned of danger, for he failed to put in an appearance and Mr Hare and his constables went disappointed away.

Margaret Byrne, Joe Byrne's mother.

15
FRUITLESS EFFORTS

IN addition to the regular police several detectives were employed by the Government in the search for the Kellys, and they travelled the country from end to end, never actually meeting the outlaws but occasionally obtaining reliable information as to their movements. The difficulty was, however, that, if not when the information was received, at least by the time it could be communicated, the Kellys were probably miles away from the spot where they have been seen; and the dangers and hardships the detectives underwent led to no particular result beyond the very useful one of making the police acquainted with the character and sentiments towards them and the outlaws of people throughout the district. The service was certainly one of considerable danger, for any detective who might be discovered was extremely likely to get a bullet through him when wandering in some remote locality. Detective Ward, who had been enquiring into the Kellys' movements before they murdered the police, and who had furnished the information on which Kennedy's party set out, was in the habit of travelling through the Kelly country in various disguises, appearing sometimes as a miner—at others as a farm hand, a stockman, a selector in search of land—and in all his journeys he succeeded in escaping recognition.

Both the Kellys and the police lived and moved and had their being in perpetual distrust of many of the men on whom they had to depend, and the distrust on both sides seems to have been justified. Several of the police agents besides Sherritt played the part of friends of the Kellys. It was, in fact, their ability to do so that gave them their chief value as agents, but while they took money from and professed to help both sides, there was reason to suspect that they did help the outlaws at least as much as the police.

Being paid by the latter for information furnished, they sometimes concocted imaginary tales, and at others gave true intelligence when it was too stale to be of any use. They probably realised that with the capture of the Kellys their occupation would be gone, and that, though some part of the reward might come into their hands, it would be impossible to them to take blood money and afterwards live in safety in the North-Eastern District.

All these agents were known to the police by assumed names, which were used in addressing them or conducting correspondence. One named

"Sherrington," who offered his services to Captain Standish, in order to prove his zeal, promptly brought in a circumstantial tale of meeting Ned Kelly and Steve Hart in the Strathbogie Ranges. Ned Kelly, he said, was very well-dressed, with beautifully polished boots, and stuck all over with revolvers. He compared watches with "Sherrington" and complimented him upon the excellent time kept by his watch. Mr Sadlier believed the story to be pure invention; but it was no use to pay agents and refuse to act upon their information, and accordingly two or three search parties were sent out without discovering the Kellys, or any trace of them. Other trouble with the agents arose through the zeal of a few law-abiding persons and some of the police, unaware of their vocation. Aaron Sherritt, especially, was a thorn in the agents' side, for warnings against him were constantly brought to Mr Hare, and once he was arrested for the theft of a horse which he stole from Mrs Byrne and sold to Ned Kelly's sister, Mr. Skillion. To Mr Hare he admitted the theft, which he had committed partly for amusement and to keep his hand in, and partly because he was not pleased with Mrs Byrne's conduct towards him and felt a desire to punish her. It would have been very annoying for the police to have their most valued agent imprisoned for horse-stealing, and accordingly when he was arrested at a later date it was contrived that not enough evidence should be brought forward to commit him for trial. To whatever extent Sherritt kept faith with the police it is certain that he was a most slippery customer. With one of Mr Hare's troopers, who was of the larrikin type, he became most "chummy." The trooper, not being in uniform, was suspected as a dangerous character by people who saw him ride into Beechworth with Aaron Sherritt, and Mr Hare received warnings against him, with a description of the fine horse he rode and was supposed to have stolen. To this trooper, just after the Jerilderie robbery, Sherritt proposed a little scheme.

The outlaws, he said, would be sure to come to Mrs Byrne's, and Joe Byrne would be leading a pack horse with the treasure strapped upon it. When the gang were fired upon by the police, the pack horse, Aaron said, would be certain to break away. The obviously sensible thing for himself and the constable to do was to follow the horse, get the pack, and hide it in the bush, returning when the excitement was over to get their "plant" and slip away with it. The trooper professed to fall in with this plan and reported it to Mr Hare, but as the outlaws did not put in an appearance nothing came of it.

After the break-up of Mr Hare's watch camp at the Byrnes' he spent his time almost continuously on shorter expeditions, sparing neither himself nor his horses nor men in his efforts to come upon the outlaws. To keep some kind of surveillance over the numerous sympathisers was in itself a formidable task, for their numbers were recruited again by the release, on April 22, of those arrested in the beginning of January and kept illegally in prison for nearly three months. The women, however, who had never been arrested, gave the most trouble. Mrs Skillion and Kate Kelly, well aware that they were being watched every night, before going to bed took out their dogs, and beat the bush for hundreds of yards round the house in search of constables, whom they sometimes discovered, shamefaced and shivering, waiting for the visitors of whose arrival there was no further chance that night. To abate the dog nuisance Mr Hare ordered his men to drop poisoned baits about the place, but the Kelly women were not to be beaten thus, and promptly put muzzles on their dogs. On one occasion Kate Kelly was seen riding away with a large bundle on the saddle to her cousin Tom Lloyd's, and was supposed to be conveying clothes or provisions to her brothers, who, it was reported, would visit Lloyd's next day. A police party accompanied by Sherritt went from Benalla, and arrived before daylight next morning near Lloyd's house which they watched from a clump of trees. Just at daybreak a boy issued from the house with dogs, which scented the police and led the boy so close to them that he must have discovered their hiding place. At any rate he ran back to the house and several shots were fired, which were probably intended to warn any of the outlaws who might be hiding in the vicinity to defer their visit to their cousin till the coast was clear.

While the Kelly sisters and cousins were most active in their assistance to the gang, and were supposed to be the chief mediums through whom news of police movements gathered by the numerous agents was communicated to the outlaws, Hart and Byrne also had brothers and sisters who spent much of their time riding about the country in the supposed interest of the outlaws. After the break up of the watch party near her mother's house, Miss Byrne, probably suspecting Sherritt, broke off her engagement with him, and he informed Mr Hare that he was going to make love to Kate Kelly. She was well disposed towards him; but Mrs Skillion, who was keener sighted, strongly objected to her sister having anything to do with Sherritt, and on one occasion, on returning to her house and finding Kate and Aaron had gone out walking together, she rode away to the Oxley police station, distant about ten miles, and laid some charge against him. She had no difficulty in showing cause why Aaron should be arrested, and a constable immediately set out to the Kellys' house to capture him. Sherritt, however, bolted when he saw the trooper coming, and though a couple of shots were fired after him succeeded in getting away to Beechworth where he reported the matter to

Detective Ward, asking him to get Mr Hare to prevent the police interfering with him, and this was done.

Mrs Skillion appears to have shown great feminine ingenuity in worrying the police. For a long time her midnight expeditions had been known to them, and in the small hours one morning, seeing her leave the house with a large bundle strapped to the saddle, a party followed her stealthily on foot, and as they believed unobserved, for miles to a gap in the hills. Day was just breaking as they climbed the hill, and at the top they found Mrs Skillion, sitting on a log waiting for them. She saluted the police by putting her fingers expressively to her nose, and when they examined the pack upon her saddle they found it contained nothing more incriminating that an old table-cloth, evidently carried away into the bush for the express purpose of taking a rise out of the police.

For months the police searched and researched the mountains, sometimes acting on information, sometimes working on a chance, and an interesting volume might be written descriptive of their experiences in the bush, but in no case did they get a glimpse of the Kellys. Mr Hare, who was the life and soul of these expeditions, some years before his death published a book, which devoted many pages to accounts of this work, and yet he declares that he "has not given a hundredth part of what actually took place during the time that he was searching for the outlaws." He, however, mentions very many incidents which space forbids enumerating here. One occasion to which he refers was productive of more than passing effect upon the fortunes of the police, since it caused or aggravated a spirit of ill-feeling between Captain Standish and the Queensland officer, Mr O'Connor, which seriously hampered the operations of the police. Captain Standish, as has been mentioned, had a low opinion of the usefulness of the trackers under Mr O'Connor's command, and one evening, when very important information arrived from a well-to-do farmer, describing carefully a locality where he had seen four men on the previous evening, and where he supposed them still to be, Captain Standish determined to go in pursuit without assistance from Mr O'Connor and the blacks.

On May 24, when the letter arrived, Captain Standish and Mr O'Connor were absent from the hotel in Benalla where the three officers lived together, but Mr Hare, who opened all the Commissioner's correspondence, read it, and was so much impressed by the writer's certainty that the men seen by him were the Kellys that he at once sent a message to the house where Captain Standish was dining, asking him to return. The Commissioner, who arrived within a few minutes, also considered the information excellent and talked over plans with Mr Hare, telling him to at once see the men and arrange for an early start next morning. In the course of the evening Mr O'Connor, too, returned to the hotel, and, addressing Mr Hare, asked, "What is the news?" Mr Hare nodded towards Captain Standish, as though referring Mr O'Connor to him, and Mr O'Connor repeated the question, but Captain Standish refused to tell him anything, having previously instructed Mr Hare also to preserve secrecy. Mr O'Connor naturally felt very much aggrieved by this rebuff, as up to this time all the officers had treated one another confidentially, whereas afterwards bitterness and jealousy arose, in which Mr Hare as well as the Commissioner became involved with Mr O'Connor.

Mr Hare, however, by no means shared Captain Standish's poor opinion of the trackers' value, and on this occasion borrowed from Mr O'Connor one of the "boys" when he started away with his party at six o'clock next morning. As for the expedition, it ended as all the others had done, in nothing. The police on leaving Benalla encountered a man named Nolan, one of the most noted Kelly sympathisers, who watched them intently, but as Mr Hare was then travelling directly away from the spot he eventually meant to visit he chuckled to himself, believing that for once the Kelly agents were outwitted. For the night he remained at a camping-place in the Warby Ranges, having made arrangements for a start at one o'clock in the morning. The men were in high spirits at the prospect of meeting the outlaws, and cheerfully submitted to resting on the bare ground without a fire—an experience in the frosty highlands by no means pleasant but by this time very familiar to them. The way to the hut where the Kellys were expected to be lay across the railway line; and there was the usual delay in opening the railways gates at the crossing. The gatekeepers, Mr Hare found, were always very hard to wake when police were on the move, and their sleepiness he put down to sympathy with the Kellys. Just before dawn the police surrounded the house. Mr Hare knocked at the door, whereupon the owner of the hut, a man named Cleary appeared, and the police officer demanded whether he had any strangers on the premises. Very hesitatingly he admitted that he had, and the police, rushing in, discovered Nolan, the agent whom they had encountered when they were making away from the house the day before. He said he had visited Clearly to give him news of a funeral at which his presence was desired, but seemed somewhat vague as to where the funeral was to be. In his turn he asked what brought the police. Mr Hare told him the tracker had followed his tracks, and Nolan expressed polite wonder at the tracker's powers of working in the dark.

This expedition is typical of many others in which the same high hopes, careful preparation, and prompt action were followed by the same lame and impotent conclusion; but very often there were added great hardship and fatigue from riding long journeys through mountainous country, and spending days and even weeks at a time in the bush, without the comfort of a fire on freezing nights when the mercury was down in the twenties.

In some respects the Kellys at this period must have had even a harder time than the police. Far out in the mountain valleys of the King and the Dandongadale, where they spent a portion of their time, they were fairly safe from attack, and were able to indulge in fires and such other comforts as a bush camp affords, but apart from the necessity of renewing their stores of food, they had a craving for the society of their friends in the more inhabited districts round Beechworth and Greta, which they could only gratify at great risk. There is no doubt that they did so and that they spent many a stolen evening by the firesides of their sympathisers, but when in a radius of some twenty miles from Benalla they lived the life of hunted animals, always ready to run or stand at bay when the slightest sound gave them warning. They were younger and hardier men than Mr Hare and many of his troopers and able to stand the wear and tear under which Mr Hare's health and spirits at length gave way. He told Captain Standish that he was no longer fit for active duty and confessed himself beaten for the time, with the result that at the beginning of July he was relieved of command in the district which was reassumed by Mr Nicolson, and almost immediately afterwards he returned to duty at the police depot in Melbourne. Very shortly before this, Captain Standish himself had gone back to the Commissioner's office in Melbourne. His presence in the North-East had contributed nothing material to any of the work done there. By his age and the fact that he had been engaged for many years in purely office work he was quite unfitted to take part in any active operations. His quarrel with Mr O'Connor prevented full use being made of the services of the trackers, and by all the officers under him, including even Mr Hare who showed no want of gratitude for the favour his chief bestowed on him, he was considered apathetic. His heart did not seem to be in the work of capturing the outlaws.

He was essentially a club-man, and his assumption of command at Benalla was said to have been an unwilling concession to the opinion of Mr Berry, then at the head of the Government, who had declared that, in Captain Standish's place, he would go to the North-Eastern District and refuse to leave it until the outlaws were taken, dead or alive.

Senior Constable Tom King (Standing); Troopers Jimmy, Hero and Barney and Victorian Police Superintendent J. Sadlier. Front Row L-R: Queensland Sub- Inspector Stanhope O'Connor, Troopers Johnny and Jack and Victoria Police Commissioner, Captain Frederick Charles Standish (hands in pockets)

16
A CHANGE IN THE PLAN OF CAMPAIGN

ONE of the first matters of Mr Nicolson's decision when he returned to the command at Benalla, arose on a question from Mr Sadlier concerning search parties sent out on chance. Mr Sadlier said "he hoped to Heaven Mr Nicolson was not going to continue this fooling any longer," to which Mr Nicolson replied that he was not. Mr Sadlier had frequently protested to Mr Hare against these expeditions which he thought wearied and broke down men and horses to no purpose, but Mr Hare refused to discontinue them. Mr Nicolson, however, was of Mr Sadlier's way of thinking and the methods of the campaign were changed. On information considered reliable and sufficiently fresh parties still went out, but the general policy adopted was, while surrounding the outlaws with spies or agents, to lull them into a sense of false security by seldom taking active measures against them. Mr Nicolson hoped that by this policy they would be tempted to show themselves with more and more boldness in the settled districts, and enable him to finally make a sudden spring which would once and for all put a stop to their career. Whether he had favoured this change or no, circumstances to some extent forced it upon him, for he was allowed to draw upon the war chest for his campaign by no means so generously as Mr Hare and Captain Standish had done. The Government were anxious to cut down expense and Captain Standish fell in with their views by withdrawing numbers of men from the district in spite of the protests of Mr Sadlier, who, having been on the spot from the beginning, was perhaps best able to judge the necessities of the situation. A comparison of the expenses incurred during Mr Hare's regime which lasted about seven months, and during that of Mr Nicholson which lasted eleven months, shows very clearly how the latter officer was relatively disadvantaged by want of money.

For the former period the expenditure was £11,371, and for the latter and longer one, only £6,722—Mr Nicolson thus having at his disposal per month less than half the money spent by Captain Standish and Mr Hare.

While numbers of police were withdrawn from the district just prior to or contemporaneously with Mr Nicolson's taking charge, the strength of the military who had been guarding townships from attack was very much reduced, 52 constables and 23 soldiers—75 men in all—being taken away from the district.

In these circumstances Mr Nicolson arranged privately with certain men of the right sort, to turn out and assist the police in case of an attack, or occasion arising for a sudden pursuit of the outlaws. At Wangaratta, Wodonga, Bright, and Mansfield, there were sufficient police to defend the banks, but not enough to make up a search party, except by combining forces or calling in the assistance of civilians. On the suggestion of Mr Sadlier a complete search party was kept always ready horsed and equipped at Benalla, but nowhere else in the district. To secure places where there was treasure from outrage and thus prevent the Kellys replenishing their coffers, and at the same time to have one efficient body to pursue them, should the apparent weakness of the police tempt them into the open, was all that Mr Nicolson felt himself able to accomplish with the resources at his command. At this time relations were more or less strained between himself and Captain Standish, with the result that Mr Nicolson believed the economies insisted on by the Commissioner were due, at least in part, to opposition to himself; and the conduct of Mr Hare, who never opposed Captain Standish, did nothing to bring about a better feeling between the officers of the police force. Mr Nicolson saw in Mr Hare a tendency to belittle his efforts and to thwart him in many petty ways, such as advising Captain Standish that ammunition was being wasted in the district, Mr Nicolson being anxious to give all the police under him increased practice, as he found many of them quite unable to make any good use of their firearms. Mr Sadlier, who seems to have possessed a fortunate faculty for keeping out of quarrels, worked loyally and amicably with whatever officer was for the time being in charge of operations, but he certainly approved the methods of Mr Nicolson far more than those of Mr Hare and Captain Standish, as did also Mr O'Connor; and when Mr Nicolson went back to the district the three officers gave each other their confidence and help in a manner forming a refreshing contrast to the state of affairs under Mr Hare.

Being limited as to money, one of Mr Nicolson's first efforts was to cut down unnecessary expense. The police had been largely using hired horses and buggies, for example, and in respect of the hire of one horse, Mr Nicolson finding a bill owing for £19 instructed Mr Sadlier to try to compromise the matter, which he did by buying the animal outright for £15, thus saving the Government £4 and getting the horse into the bargain. The police stables, too, at Benalla were another useless source of great expense, being full of highly-fed horses while there was splendid grass in the Department's paddock.

Mr Nicolson accordingly turned the horses into it, giving them an allowance of hay every day to keep them in hard condition, thus saving a considerable amount of money and giving added usefulness to the horses; for when stable fed and sheltered, at the end of a three days' expedition into the mountains they were tucked up and useless from the cold and change of feed; whereas under Mr Nicolson's system they became as well qualified as the outlaws' horses to stand hard work upon such feed as they could pick when hobbled in the bush at night.

While introducing these reforms Mr Nicolson constantly travelled about the country himself, seeing people, making friends with them, and endeavouring to gain the confidence and assistance of the farmers. The men were instructed to do likewise, and as a result information from good sources concerning the Kellys began to arrive at headquarters. At first the informants were timid, and the items of news were not communicated until they were perhaps a month old. Then only a fortnight would elapse before the people spoke, and later on there was more or less constant information coming in, sometimes not a week old. Meanwhile Mr Nicolson waited patiently. He had reason to believe that the outlaws were greatly hampered by want of money, and that their friends were urging them to make another bank raid, which, if attempted, would probably result in their capture. Some exploit was necessary to renew their prestige and furnish them with the means of buying loyalty, and at the same time the presence of the trackers whom they greatly feared, and the suspicion that their doings were watched by spies, kept them in a state of nervous unrest which it was hoped would result sooner or later in some act of rash stupidity.

During this time their lived principally within a radius of twelve miles from the Kellys' home at Greta. Police agents were watching them, but while they kept quiet Mr Nicolson would not have them disturbed unless a chase were practically certain to end in capture. Acting on this principle he let one chance go which Mr Sadlier thought should have been seized upon, though as a rule he was in perfect accord with Mr Nicolson. In Wangaratta one day Mr Sadlier received information from an agent that on the previous evening five armed men, four of whom were supposed to be the outlaws, had been seen by him near the house of Tom Lloyd, not far from Greta. He had passed them, he said, unobserved. Mr Sadlier telegraphed the information to Mr Nicolson at Benalla and advised a search. On instructions from Mr Nicolson he went by train to join the other officers at Benalla, but was unable to take with him his informant as Mr Nicolson asked him to do, since the man had been drinking and could not be found in time. On a consultation between Mr Nicolson, Mr Sadlier, and Mr O'Connor, it was decided to send out a search party before daybreak, and horses were saddled up and the men warned to be in readiness for a start at one o'clock. Mr Sadlier then went away to rest, but on his return at one o'clock found that Mr Nicolson had changed his mind and issued orders for the abandonment of the exhibition. He and Mr O'Connor had talked the matter over in Mr Sadleir's absence, and, not feeling sure of that officer's ability to find the spot, and considering, also, that it was bad stony ground for trackers to work in, while the outlaws being on foot, would leave a very poor trail, they thought under the circumstances it was wiser to make no move.

Mr Sadlier was not unnaturally annoyed, and a good deal was made of the incident by Captain Standish and others unfriendly to Mr Nicolson. He however pointed out that in addition to other reasons for inaction was the fact that the informant was the same man who had endeavoured to send the police off to the head of the King River when the outlaws were at Euroa, and one, therefore, on whom it was not safe to rely. Information was steadily improving, and an unsuccessful dash at the outlaws might have awoken them from their sense of false security, and driven them away to the distant mountain country of Tomgroggin, in New South Wales. In the cases where Mr Nicolson did take action, he made great use of the trackers, who were instrumental in finding more than one of the Kellys' deserted camps and on one occasion picked up the tracks of a man near Mrs Byrne's house, which, from the shape of the footprints, Mr Nicolson was sure were made by Joe Byrne, while other tracks indicated that the gully in which lay the Byrnes' and the Sherritts' houses had been visited by the whole gang on horseback. This evidence corroborated the information which was given from time to time by Aaron Sherritt and one of his younger brothers, who was also in the confidence of the outlaws and had now begun to bring tales of them to the police.

Joe Byrne, who was the literary man of the gang, used frequently to indulge in letter writing. One of his compositions, posted in September by young Sherritt was a threatening letter to Detective Ward and other police, warning them of mischief to happen before the end of the month, and at the outlaw's own request a notice of the letter was published in a local paper.

During September Sherritt had other interviews with Joe Byrne, who also called at his mother's house and left £2 as payment to Sherritt for services in connection with the letter. It was during this month that Mr Nicolson abandoned the proposed search near Greta, after making preparations for it.

Again in November Sherritt was in communication with the outlaws through Joe Byrne, meeting him on one occasion in the scrubby ranges near Peechelba.

Byrne's spurs were covered with blood, and he appeared to have ridden hard. He seemed to be troubled in his mind about the murder of Kennedy and hinted at another projected bank robbery, trying to persuade Sherritt to join the gang as a scout. Shortly after this the outlaws apparently grew suspicious of Sherritt, for Dan Kelly called at the Sherritts' house and searched it with a revolver in his hand, but without finding the agent who was working in a paddock nearby. On hearing of Dan Kelly's visit he hid himself until dark, and then rode into Beechworth and told Mr Nicolson who happened to be there.

Sherritt was instructed to conceal his fear of the gang and endeavour to remain on good terms with them, which he did, and soon Joe Byrne again visited him at his hut. He thanked him for his services in posting various letters and putting up in different places certain caricatures of the police, and also mentioned that he and Ned were discussing rival plans for sticking up one of the Beechworth banks. His own was to visit a bank at night when the manager was in bed, and he did not care if blood were shed over it. He looked worried and was very thin. Their horses, he said, were poor, but his own grey was still the best. A woman who was in the party suggested that he should give himself up and turn informer against the others in the hope of a pardon, but he refused, saying that people would say that he was worse than Sullivan (a former notorious murderer and bushranger who gave Queen's evidence) and hunt him out of the colony.

On this information the police took special measures to protect the Beechworth banks, and Mr Nicolson established a watch party in a cave above Mrs Sherritt's house. The existence of this party, he believed, was an absolute secret in the district, but Mr Hare heard of it at the Melbourne Depot from a constable who must have been in communication with one of its members, and Mr Hare spoke of it to Captain Standish, telling him that everyone knew where Mr Nicolson's men were concealed. Accordingly, Captain Standish, who frequently visited Benalla, worried Mr Nicolson much about the matter, and finally ordered him to withdraw the cave party after it had been out some weeks unknown, so Mr Nicolson still believed, to the outlaws, and likely to surprise them in the gully at any time. Since Mr Nicolson had been in charge he was aware that the Kellys' sisters were constantly making purchases of stores in Benalla, which he believed were for the outlaws' use, and which were paid for by Bank of New South Wales notes with an earthy smell, suggesting that they had been buried somewhere to conceal them. It was practically certain that they were part of the proceeds of the Jerilderie robbery, but nothing could be proved, and though it was also known that Mrs Skillion and one of the Lloyds bought large quantities of ammunition at a leading Melbourne gun shop no steps were taken against them. The ammunition purchased was clearly intended for the Kellys' use, as it was for the kind needed for the Spencer rifles taken from Kennedy's party and another more modern make of rifle taken from the New South Wales police at Jerilderie. The train in which Lloyd and Mrs Skillion travelled was on one occasion searched, but no ammunition was found. They had either thrown it from the window at a spot which they could visit later, or left it behind to be forwarded by another train.

At the beginning of the new year Mr Nicolson had good reason to believe that the outlaws were getting near the end of their tether. Reports came to hand that they were growing thin and wearied from anxiety and fatigue. Owing to fear of the trackers they very seldom rode, but went on foot to places where their horses were brought to them when they wished to make a move. By day they concealed themselves in the long grass and rushes by the Greta swamp and prowled about at night, in their desire to avoid recognition seldom even carrying their rifles. Mr Nicolson and Mr Sadlier were well satisfied with the work of the last six months, and though there were complaints in the press from time to time about their failure to capture the Kellys, knowing what they did, they kept their own counsel. For many months, in spite of reduced police strength, the Kellys had not ventured upon outrage of any kind, and the officers saw good reason to hope that early in 1880 would come about the downfall of the gang.

The Death of Aaron Sherritt.

17
AARON SHERRITT'S DEATH

ABOUT the middle of April, 1880, Mr Nicolson received notice that he was to be superseded in the command. Naturally this information was most mortifying to him, as he expected that his labours were shortly going to have fruition, and he felt very bitter against Captain Standish, who, he considered, had belittled his efforts and hampered him in many ways in his work, and now recommended his recall. He immediately went to Melbourne, had some warm words with the Chief Commissioner, and on urgent appeal to the Chief Secretary, Mr. Ramsay, obtained an extension of time until the end of May. Matters were growing worse and worse for the outlaws. All their horses were knocked up and most of them abandoned. Their friends, disappointed by their inactivity, were grumbling, and urging that they must "do" another bank in order to reward the faithful. They seldom dared to appear together, and their active aids and assistants were said to be reduced to about four, while the people willing to inform against were growing in numbers. During April the watch party had been removed from the cave near Mrs Byrne's and there were reports that the outlaws again sometimes visited her. In February Mr Nicolson had learnt of the theft of plough-shares and mouldboards from several farms in the neighbourhood of Oxley, about nine miles from Wangaratta, and on May 20 he received a letter giving a startling explanation of the theft. This letter is worth quotation as an example of the terms in which the agents wrote to the police whom they addressed by fictitious names, while also using assumed signatures themselves. This agent—usually known among the police as "the diseased stock" man—since this description of the outlaws was always used in correspondence with him, in his assumed character as an inspector of stock wrote as follows:

"Greta, May 20, 1880. Mr. William Charles Balfour, Benalla. Dear Sir,—Nothing definite re the diseased stock of this locality. I have made careful inspection, but did not find (sic) exact source of disease. I have seen and spoke to —— and —— on Tuesday, who were fencing near home. All others I have not been able to see. Missing portions of cultivators, described as jackets, are now being worked and fit splendidly. Tested previous to using, and proof at ten yards. I shall be in Wangaratta on Monday, before when I may learn how to treat the disease. I am perfectly satisfied that it is where last indicated, but in what region I can't discover. A break out may be anticipated, as feed is getting very scarce. Five are now bad. I will post a note giving any bad symptoms I may perceive from Wangaratta on Monday and Tuesday at latest, and will wait on you for news how to proceed on a day which I shall then state, before end of the week. Other animals are, I fear, diseased. Yours faithfully, B.C.W."

The gist of this communication is that the stolen portions of the ploughs were being converted into armour for the Kellys. That it fitted splendidly, and was proof against bullets at a range of ten yards. Also that a break out on the part of the outlaws might be very shortly expected.

When Mr Nicolson received this news he had only about a week longer to spend in the district and he employed it as actively as possible, among other things arranging to have a watch kept on the Glenrowan hotel where the Kelly sympathisers had taken to gathering and indulging in disorderly conduct. He also paid a visit to Mrs Sherritt, from whom he learnt that she had lately seen Joe Byrne, and that he had told her they "could go anywhere if it were not for her sanguinary son." Thereupon he determined on one more effort to catch the outlaws in that neighbourhood, and arranged that a party of police should be sent to live in concealment in the house of Aaron Sherritt, who had been recently married to a Beechworth girl and was living with his wife at his old quarters in the gully at Woolshed.

On June 1 Mr Nicolson's connection with the Kelly pursuit finally ceased, Mr Hare coming up to Benalla to take over the charge of affairs. His supersession was a bitter pill to Mr Nicolson, more especially as he felt that he had been misrepresented by Captain Standish and to some extent by Mr Hare. The meeting between the two officers was therefore not particularly cordial, though outwardly friendly relations were maintained, and at the police office in Benalla Mr Nicolson gave to the new leader a rough outline of what he had been doing and what he had hoped to do.

This conversation took place in Mr Sadlier's presence, and when, at a later date, Mr Hare accused Mr Nicolson of having withheld information from him, and of having treated him in a grudging spirit, Mr Sadlier emphatically asserted that he considered the accusation most unjust. Mr Nicolson, in his opinion, had told Mr Hare all it was possible to tell in the time, and he himself, being perfectly acquainted with all the work, was in a position to supply any details that had been overlooked. Mr Hare, who had an unfortunately keen eye for faults in his brother officers, also made it a subject of complaint that Mr Nicolson had withdrawn police from watch parties and dismissed all the agents without giving him (Mr Hare) notice of his action; but on enquiry, a telegram from Mr Nicolson to one of the senior constables was produced, in which it was stated that all further orders were to come from Superintendents Sadlier or Hare, and that Detective Ward had instructions that no further authority or supplies for the agents were available. From this it seemed clear that Mr Nicolson only intended, in a business-like way, to terminate his own responsibility for the payment of agents and the movements of them or the police, leaving Mr Hare unhampered, to make his own arrangements. When the substitution of Mr Hare for Mr Nicolson was first mooted, Mr Sadlier had written to the former, urging him, as a friend in the strong terms, not to accept the command in Mr Nicolson's place. He wrote entirely in the public interest, believing that Mr Nicolson's tactics were likely to soon bear fruit in success, while he did not believe in Mr Hare's. To do Mr Hare justice, he did himself protest strongly against being sent to take command, saying he had tried once to catch the outlaws and failed; but he based his main objections to undertaking the work upon the score of his age and state of health, and urged that there were other officers in the force senior to him who should be sent to try their hands. He, however, expressed himself in such an unfortunate manner that to some of these senior officers it appeared that he was casting a slur upon their courage, and suggesting unwillingness on their part to undertake a difficult and dangerous duty, while he did not rise to the generosity of putting in a good word for Mr Nicolson who had begged to retain the command a little longer. Mr Hare's protests had no effect. Captain Standish and Mr Ramsay both considered him the best man for the duty. He was told that the public were growing more and more indignant at the outlaws' long unchecked career, and, with *carte blanche* in everything, he went up in obedience to orders and threw himself heartily into the work.

Mr Sadlier, in spite of his disapproval of the change, supported Mr Hare loyally. Mr O'Connor and his trackers very shortly left the district for Melbourne, for Mr Hare considered that while they remained at Benalla the outlaws would be afraid to come into the open, and the Queensland Government, which considered that their officer had not been particularly well treated, was desirous that he should bring his trackers home as soon as their services could be dispensed with.

After some days spent in reading up the correspondence and other office work Mr Hare personally interviewed and re-engaged most of Mr Nicolson's agents, and re-established a party of four police in Aaron Sherritt's house. Aaron had been somewhat under a cloud in Mr Hare's absence. He did not get on well with Mr Nicolson who showed rather contemptuous distrust of him; but he brightened up on the return of his old friend, who shook hands with him and scolded him for his past laziness and sulks. Aaron said he would do better in future, and promised to give his most loyal endeavours to the work of betraying his former associates to death.

In addition to the police at Sherritt's house Mr Hare sent out other parties, setting one of four constables to watch the Kellys' house where Mrs Skillion lived at Greta, and another of the same number to watch the Harts' house near Wangaratta. He was aware that the outlaws were now almost entirely dependent for supplies upon their blood relations who would desert them in no extremity. The watching was skilfully managed, Mr Hare's instructions being that after nightfall the constables should go, one by one, from the police stations at Wangaratta or Glenrowan to their respective rendezvous, and keep the houses under observation all night, returning singly as they had gone in order not to excite comment should they be seen.

While a net was thus being woven round the outlaws there were signs of great unrest among their sympathisers. They were all excited and some jubilant—declaring that the Kellys would shortly do a deed that should astonish not only Australia but the whole world.

Sooner even than the police expected the end came—or the beginning of the end—and with dramatic suddenness. On the night of Saturday, June 26, Anton Wicks, a German miner, who lived not far from Aaron Sherritt's house, was encountered by two horsemen just as darkness was coming on. One of them led another horse. He did not know them at first, but when they spoke he recognised Joe Byrne with whom he had been long acquainted. Byrne and Dan Kelly, who was his companion, bailed up Anton Wicks, and, putting handcuffs upon him, commanded him under pain of being immediately shot to go with them to Aaron Sherritt's dwelling for a purpose which they would explain to him on the way.

Sherritt's little house was crowded that evening. The four constables were there, waiting till it should be time to go upon their nightly watch at Mrs Byrne's, and in addition there were Aaron and his wife, and her mother, Mrs Barry, who had come to spend an evening with her daughter.

Tea was over and it was only just dark when the inmates of the house heard footsteps outside, and a knock at the door followed. Aaron asked who was there, and Wicks answered him. Mrs Sherritt went to the door, then turning to her husband she said, "It is Anton Wicks. He has lost his way."

For a moment Aaron seemed to hesitate. Then he walked to the door, asking again, "Who is that?" and seeing it was really Wicks, said a word or two jokingly, before beginning to direct him to his home.

Suddenly there came a flash out of the darkness, a report, and Joe Byrne stepped forward from among the trees. He had shot Sherritt, who was staggering backwards, and coming closer Byrne fired again. The bullet almost touched Mrs Sherritt, who was standing by her husband and shrank aside; but it struck him in the body and he fell upon the floor without a word. A bright fire was burning in the kitchen which formed one half the Sherritts' hut. Three police were in the bedroom which formed the other half, and the fourth constable entered it through a door in the partition just as Wicks and Byrne came to the house. Mrs Barry, the murdered man's mother-in-law, knelt upon the floor beside him and saw that he was dying, while her daughter rushed distracted into the bedroom. Joe Byrne stood over Mrs Barry, almost touching the body that lay by the doorway, and he threatened to put a ball through her unless she told him who was in the house. Apparently he had heard the constable go into the bedroom when he came to the entrance of the hut, but he obtained nothing from Mrs Barry beyond that there was a man looking for work, and glancing at Aaron he said, "I wanted that fellow. I have got him now and I am satisfied."

Meanwhile, the police in the bedroom were in a wretched state of excitement and fear, uncertain what to do, and doing nothing beyond clutching their firearms and whispering together. A manly rush upon Byrne, when for a few seconds he stood by the door after firing his shot, might have settled the outlaw and saved them from disgrace, but they let the moment go by. Their justification was that in the hurry and the darkness they could not soon enough obtain their rifles.

Afterwards the man stepped back into darkness, and when the police looked over the partition dividing the kitchen from the bedroom there was no one to be seen. Immediately after the shot was fired, they heard Mrs Sherritt cry out:

"Oh, Joe, what did you shoot poor Aaron for?" and the answer, "The —— will never put me away again." They knew at last they had met the Kellys for whom they had been seeking so long, and the only thought among them was how best to keep a whole skin.

Strangely enough the outlaws do not seem to have known that there were police in the house. Joe Byrne made Mrs Barry open the front door of the kitchen. It was the back to which Byrne and Wicks had come, and standing outside on either side of the house they called on the men, whoever they might be, to come out and be killed "like —— dogs." They fired several shots into the house, by way of encouragement, but still the police did not stir, and still the women who ran backwards and forwards, and were constantly threatened with death unless they confessed who was in the house, would say nothing but that they were men looking for work.

In the bedroom the constables still whispered together, and allowed each to persuade the other that it would be madness to venture out—that if they held the place they would do well. A rush would certainly have involved a risk to life for the outlaws were in the darkness, and before the constables could reach the open they would have been exposed to fire through either door of the kitchen, which was brightly lighted by the burning logs on the hearth. It was a risk they were not prepared to run, and to further protect themselves they hit upon a brilliant idea. Mrs Sherritt had been running distractedly in and out of the bedroom, and once when she came they kept her with them and forced her to get under the bed. She would be safer there, they said—and so would they—for while women were in the room they trusted that the outlaws would not fire through the weatherboard walls. Mrs Barry, indeed, begged them not to, saying that they would shoot her daughter, and they fired no more, but spoke of setting alight to the house and actually tried to do so, placing brushwood against the walls and striking matches, which went out.

Here one would suppose came chance for a rush, while at least one of the murderers was engaged in trying to fire the house, but the constables and the women believed all the outlaws to be there, and they resorted to strategy.

Mrs Barry was called into the bedroom, and, partly by persuasion and partly by force, detained there, for the constables considered that the outlaws would not be such cowardly brutes as to burn down the house while there were women in it.

Some hours after the abortive or pretended attempt to burn the house the outlaws departed, but at what hour was not ascertained, for the police remained in the house till the morning when a Chinaman who was passing was persuaded to take a letter to a schoolmaster, who, in his turn, visited the house and took information of the murder to Beechworth. People gradually collected round the murdered man's dwelling and by two o'clock in the afternoon a large crowd had collected, but the constables still held the house and refused to admit anyone till the arrival of Mr. Foster, a police magistrate from Beechworth, to whom they shortly explained the facts of the affair.

18
THE PRISONERS AT GLENROWAN

IT was about one o'clock on Sunday afternoon when a telegram with the news of Sherritt's murder reached Mr Hare at Benalla. Since the outlaws had broken out once more they needed no longer to be encouraged by the black trackers' absence, and Mr Hare therefore wired to Captain Standish to send them up immediately by special train to Beechworth. Mr O'Connor and his men had then retired from their temporary Victorian service and were to leave in a few days for Queensland. A request by wire from Captain Standish to the Queensland Commissioner for permission to send them again on duty was refused, but Mr Ramsay, the Victorian Chief Secretary, intervened, and pointing out the urgency of the case, obtained authority from the Queensland Government for Mr O'Connor to act with the Victorian police. Mr Ramsay therefore wired to Mr Hare that he would send the men up next morning, and Mr Hare, with pardonable irritation, replied that if they did not start that night they need no come at all. Thereupon matters were expedited a little and a special train, with Mr O'Connor, some lady relatives, his black trackers and several pressmen, was despatched from Melbourne for Benalla, en route for Beechworth, about half an hour after midnight.

During the day Mr Hare was kept more or less in forced idleness, waiting for the trackers and the men. He greatly regretted that poor Sherritt, who had been married only six months or more, had fallen a victim to his zeal in assisting the police. There was a certain retributive justice in his suffering vengeance from the men he had betrayed, but to Mr Hare he had always been a faithful and active assistant, and with all his faults he seems to have won regard from many people who knew him, while his wife and his old mother were overwhelmed by grief at his death.

Meanwhile Dan Kelly and Joe Byrne, allowing their decoy, Anton Wicks, to slip away to his home, had left Sherritts' hut sometime after midnight on Saturday and ridden hard across country to the township of Glenrowan, distant about forty miles from the scene of the murder. At Glenrowan, which lies on the main Sydney line, nearly midway between Wangaratta to the north and Benalla to the south, Ned Kelly and Steve Hart had already established themselves in undisputed possession. The township was a small one, consisting of little more than hotels and the school-house, store and blacksmith's shop which compose the nucleus of so many Australian bush hamlets, but near the railway station there were in addition the residences of the stationmaster and one or two other railway employees.

The methods of the gang were, in the main, of the same character as those pursued at Euroa or Jerilderie; but in this case there was no bank to be robbed, and they suited their conduct to the particular end in view. This was the destruction of the railway line at a point some distance on the Wangaratta side of Glenrowan, where a sharp curve would hide the torn up rails from the view of the engine-driver of a train coming from Melbourne until the locomotive was upon them. Just there the line ran upon a steep embankment, and an accident would have disastrous consequences, which the Kellys intended to aggravate by pouring in a hot fire upon the struggling survivors. It was a cold-blooded and well-laid scheme, showing in its conception an accurate forecast of the probable movements of the police. The day being Sunday no ordinary trains would be passing along the line for many hours, and Ned Kelly felt sure that on the news of Sherritt's murder being wired to Melbourne a police special would be immediately sent up. He even seems to have calculated on Mr Hare asking for the return of the black trackers, for they were the men on whom he specially wanted to wreak his vengeance for the hunted life his gang had led so long.

Very early on Sunday morning Hart and Kelly called at the house of the Glenrowan stationmaster, for the purpose of getting him or others to tear up the rails. Mr Stannistreet, the stationmaster, professed that he knew nothing of such things; therefore, leaving Hart to keep guard over Mr Stanistreet, his family, and other prisoners whom they had collected, Ned Kelly obtained the services of some plate-layers, whom he forced to do the work. One of them, a man named Reardon, begged to be let off the task, but Ned Kelly, saying he soon expected a train with police and those — — blacks, threatened to tickle him up with a revolver if he did not do it, and do it quickly. Kelly wanted four rails' lengths of the line broken, but Reardon assured him that one length was as good as twenty, for he had some faint hope that if only one rail were taken the engine might leap it and go safely on.

When the line was broken Kelly drove the railway men to join the other prisoners at the railway station, later on transferring them all to Mrs Jones's hotel. This hotel, which stood among trees about two hundred yards from the railway platform, and facing it, was a weatherboard building, with a verandah in front into which opened the bar, and for the rest consisted of several small rooms with a passage running through from the front to the back.

Before the prisoners arrived it seems that several of the Kelly sympathisers were in the place, which for some time previously had been with them a popular house of call. During Sunday the prisoners, whose number was added to from time to time until it totalled sixty-two, made themselves as comfortable as they could and many of them spent a merry time. No one appears to have noticed at what hour Dan Kelly and Byrne arrived from Beechworth, and nothing was said of Sherritts' murder, but the four outlaws were in the hotel together throughout the day. Mrs Jones, the proprietress of the establishment, seemed to rather relish having such a full house, and was in every way anxious to please her outlawed visitors. Though it was Sunday the bar was not kept closed, and a good deal of liquor was consumed, but the outlaws, on the whole, were temperate. Hart in the morning drank too much, but the effects wore off, and later on in the day he kept sober, while, when Dan Kelly poured out a stiff nobbler of brandy, someone heard a warning, "Steady, old man!" from Joe Byrne.

Among the prisoners confined in the hotel was a Mr Curnow, the local State schoolmaster, who was bailed up by Ned Kelly at eleven o'clock in the morning when taking his wife and family for a drive. He seems to have made a favourable impression on the outlaws who treated him politely, Dan Kelly going so far as to seek him where he was standing in the yard at about one o'clock in the day with an invitation to come and dance. Curnow said he was afraid he could not do much without dancing boots and asked Kelly to go with him to his house to get them, suggesting, also, that he should be allowed to leave his family at home. He knew that he would have to pass by the police-station, where he hoped the constable, Bracken, might be warned of the Kellys' presence in time to ride away with the news. Ned Kelly was inclined to consent but Dan objected to his leaving the place, so Mr Curnow was obliged to dance in his ordinary boots. He had heard of the Kelly plan of wrecking the police train, and with the object of getting free and possibly averting disaster he worked hard to further ingratiate himself with the outlaws. Happening to learn that one of his fellow prisoners had a revolver in his possession, he called Ned Kelly aside and informed him of the fact. Ned Kelly thanked him, and was gulled into the belief that Curnow was devoted to his interests—a belief which was strengthened when at nine o'clock in the evening the outlaws were about to go to the police station to capture Bracken, the constable already referred to. Curnow had heard Ned Kelly talking of the matter to Mrs Jones, and he suggested that it would be wise to take his (Curnow's) brother-in-law, Dave Mortimer, to the barracks to call Bracken out, since the constable would know his voice and come unsuspectingly into the outlaw's power. Ned Kelly approved of this idea, and on the strength of of the help he had given Curnow asked leave to depart from the hotel and go to his home with his wife and sister, who were then at the house of the stationmaster, Mr Stanistreet, which had been used as a place of detention for some of the women. Curnow assured Kelly that there was no need to distrust him as he was with the outlaws heart and soul, to which Kelly replied, "Yes; I know that, and I can see it."

The schoolmaster was then allowed to bring his women- folk to the hotel, where they waited for some time, wondering whether they would be allowed to go. Ned Kelly and Byrne were discussing matters in a room which they had reserved to themselves. Some of the prisoners were gathered round a fire of logs which they had lit in the hotel yard while others were playing cards in the hotel, all seemingly content with their position and anxious to amuse themselves as the outlaws had instructed them to do. Towards ten o'clock in the evening Ned Kelly directed Curnow to put his horse into his buggy and drive round to the front of the hotel, telling him to take with him a little boy, the son of the Glenrowan postmaster, as well as the two ladies. After waiting some time, Curnow was joined by Kelly and Byrne on horseback, wearing overcoats, with bundles strapped in front of them, carrying rifles in their hands, and presenting a peculiarly bulky appearance which Curnow was at a loss to account for. They were escorting Dave Mortimer on horseback, and two of the prisoners who resided with the postmaster on foot, all these being intended as hostages or decoys to assist in the capture of Bracken. Knocking and calling failed to bring him out of the barracks, and after searching the place Kelly took Alec Reynolds, the postmaster's little boy, out of Curnow's buggy, going with him and Mr E. Reynolds, another of the prisoners into the postmaster's yard. Outside the yard the Curnows had a long and anxious wait under the eye of Joe Byrne, and it was nearly an hour later when Kelly came out again with Bracken and the others, leading Bracken's horse. He order the constable to mount and led the horse with a halter, remarking that he could not trust Bracken with the bridle, to which Bracken replied that had he not been ill in bed all day Kelly would not have captured him so easily. Kelly then told Curnow he might drive home, directing him to go to bed, and warning him significantly not to dream too loud. The outlaws and their prisoners rode away to the hotel, where a dance was in progress and everything appeared to be going merrily. During the dance Bracken, who had observed where the key of the door was placed on the mantelpiece, seized an opportunity when no one was looking of picking it up and slipping it into his boot, with a view to making his escape.

The night had nearly gone when Dan Kelly told the prisoners they might go home, and they were all making for the door, when Mrs Jones interfered, saying that before they departed, Ned Kelly wished to give them a lecture. The prisoners waited respectfully, and Ned, after a word or two of advice and moralising to some of the civilians, turned to Bracken and began to address him on the wickedness and laziness of a constable's life—a subject on which he had talked seriously to McIntyre on the day of the police murders nearly two years before.

Suddenly a whistle was heard in the distance and expectant horrified silence fell upon the crowd. Ned Kelly broke off his discourse. Byrne came in from the back room, saying, "The train is coming." Ned Kelly went out to join the others; Bracken seized the opportunity to escape, locking the door behind him when he went out, and those left in the hotel heard from the back room the rattle of iron, for the Kellys were dressing themselves in the armour made from stolen ploughshares, preparing to do battle with any of the police who might escape from the wreck of the train.

Mr. Curnow Stopping the Police Train.—

19
THE ASSAULT UPON THE HOTEL

IN getting home after his dismissal by Ned Kelly, Mr Curnow determined to execute a plan he had been nursing in his mind all day to save the train, if only he could gain his liberty in time. If possible he would make a dash for Benalla with his buggy to warn the police before they started and if too late endeavour to signal them upon the line. Mrs Curnow was almost hysterical with fear, declaring they were watched by the outlaws and that interference with their schemes would mean death to all the household. Her husband persuaded her to accompany him with his sister and the baby to her mother's house, and, to explain their absence to the outlaws, should his home be searched, he left a note, saying that they had all gone to Mrs Mortimer's to put his wife who was ill under her mother's care. Scarcely, however, had they reached Mrs Mortimer's house than Mrs Curnow's fears broke out again, and her husband dared not leave her, lest in her distracted state she should rouse suspicion in the outlaws and come to harm, and he therefore took her home again. Still he could not stand idle and see the train go to destruction. His sister, who thought as he did, took Mrs Curnow to her room, assuring her that her husband was likewise going presently to bed, and he made all haste to harness up his horse for a race to Benalla. Suddenly he heard the train approaching. It was at some distance still. Sound travelled far on the clear frosty night, but there was need for desperate haste. Leaving his buggy, Mr Curnow snatched up a candle, a red scarf, and matches which he had in readiness, and, rushing away to the railway line, ran as fast as he could between the rails in the direction of the approaching train. Early in the day he had noticed his sister wearing a red scarf. It had flashed across his mind that, with a light behind it, the scarf might be used as a danger signal, and now the test of its usefulness had come.

Trembling with anxiety lest the outlaws should shoot him down and frustrate his scheme, or that the engine driver would not heed his faint red light, he lit the candle and held the shawl in front of it. There was a long warning whistle, the engine which was bearing down upon him slowed and came to a stop a few yards from where he stood. The danger, to others at least, was over, and he had the exultation of knowing that his resource and courage had saved the occupants of the special from almost certain death.

The train had started that night from Melbourne with Mr O'Connor, his wife and sister (who meant to remain in Beechworth), pressmen and black trackers.

Due at Benalla at 12.30, it had been delayed for half an hour by smashing through a railway gate and injuring the breaks — a delay which probably was the salvation of its occupants, for half an hour earlier it would have steamed past Glenrowan unwarned. At Benalla Mr Hare was in waiting, with a body of constables and horses ready trucked, while another engine was under steam, Mr Hare intending to proceed to Beechworth and await the black trackers there if the Melbourne special should be much longer delayed. This engine it was decided to use as a pilot, and by way of further precaution against surprise Mr Hare proposed to place a man in front of the locomotive, strapped on as a security against falling, with instructions to keep a keen lookout. This plan, however, was abandoned, and with all its occupants in the highest spirits the train steamed out of Benalla, the pilot engine 150 yards in front carrying one or two of Mr Hare's men armed and watchful.

When Mr Curnow's red light brought the pilot to a standstill, the warning whistles checked the train behind, and as soon as it stopped Mr Hare with his gun in readiness, jumped down from his carriage and met the guard of the pilot engine approaching him. The signaller, he told Mr Hare, had gone, and the only news he gave was that the Kellys had pulled up the line beyond Glenrowan.

The guard had said he would go on to Glenrowan station, draw up there, and await the special which was following. Begging him for God's sake not do so, as he would certainly be shot, Curnow had then hurried away at top speed, saying he must go to his wife.

Very much in the dark as to the Kellys' movements, but believing them to be in the neighbourhood of the torn up rails, Mr Hare put more armed men upon the engines and ordered a slow advance to the station. As the trains drew up to the platform there was no sound anywhere; no one stirring, and not a sign of life, beyond a light in the window of the stationmaster's house, about a hundred yards distant from the station. With another gentleman, Mr Hare hastened to the house, where they knocked at the window, and it was opened by Mrs Stanistreet, the stationmaster's wife, who was crying, and in great distress. Only a few minutes before, her husband had been taken by the outlaws to the hotel. With some others they had kept him confined in his own house all day, so that they might force him, with a revolver at his head, to make any signal which the train might require assuring safety before running express past Glenrowan, but all chance of that happening was over, and he also had been removed to the hotel prison house. Mr Hare, however, could learn nothing from the distracted Mrs Stanistreet but that her husband had been taken away by the Kellys not ten minutes before—as Mr Hare thought into the Warby Ranges. Accordingly he returned to the station and gave orders to detrain the horses with a view to pursuit.

This work was in progress when a man appeared on the platform and besought Mr Hare to go quickly to the hotel. It was Bracken, who had just escaped, and he told of the presence of the outlaws, saying unless they were attacked immediately they would be gone. Mr Hare did not hesitate for a moment. With hasty instructions to let the horses go, calling on his men to follow him, he ran towards the hotel, crossing a fence and ditches on his way. The building was in darkness, the only light coming from the moon which was low behind the house, when suddenly there were flashes of flame from four dimly-seen figures on the verandah and bullets whistled among the police. All escaped unhit except Mr Hare who led the party, and who was struck by a bullet in the left wrist. The police returned the fire, Mr Hare using a gun with his uninjured hand, and as the sound of the first volley died away, a voice from the verandah was heard calling, "Fire away, you — —. You can do us no harm."

For a minute or two a sharp fusillade continued, fifty or sixty rifle or revolver shots being fired on either side, when the men on the verandah retreated into or round the hotel, and with a lull in the firing the police heard piteous screams of pain and terror issuing from the house. Up to that time there had been no suspicion that non-combatant men, women, and children were behind the walls through which the Martini bullets were crashing, and on the sound of their voices reaching him Mr Hare gave the order to cease fire.

After that, telling his men to surround the house, he retired to the station, faint from his wound which was bleeding profusely, and which the pressmen at the train bound up for him. Strongly dissuaded by the ladies, who had pluckily kept their places in the railway carriage, with bullets whistling past them, Mr Hare made an effort to go back to the scene of action, but the pain and the loss of blood overcame him, and he had to retire once more and remain upon the platform until the train was ready to convey him with the ladies back to Benalla. There, before having his wound dressed, Mr Hare despatched a number of telegrams, dictating them to the stationmaster, and made arrangements for reinforcements of police being sent forward to Glenrowan.

Within the hotel the unfortunate prisoners were in a pitiable state. Had the train been five minutes later they would have been spared the horrors of the fight in which they suffered, for, to do the outlaws justice, it does not seem that they counted upon or wished for safety from the presence of non-combatants among them. Had they done so they would have been sadly undeceived; but, as a matter of fact, but for Mrs Jones' unfortunate appeal for a lecture from Ned Kelly, all the prisoners would have been free before the attack began. Dan Kelly had just given them permission to depart when Ned began the address for which they waited. Then came the sound of the approaching train, and all chance of escape was gone, for, with the door locked, the outlaws went to don their armour, and, later, the people dared not venture out in the darkness in the face of a storm of bullets. The police were excited and little inclined, even were they able to distinguish friend from foe, as some of the prisoners found to their cost, and indeed the only constable in the force for whom most of them had reason to feel anything but bitterness was Constable Bracken, who before he departed gave a warning to lie close upon the floor if firing came. Altogether, Bracken's is the only name in the Victorian police force which derived any added lustre from the events of the day. He seems to have acted throughout with pluck and judgment, and not long after telling Mr Hare of the Kelly's presence he galloped away to Wangaratta to bring back further aid.

When Mr Hare had left the field the police were under no real command, for while Sub-Inspector O'Connor considered that he held it, most of the men, not recognising a Queensland officer, if they looked to anybody for direction looked to Senior- Constable Kelly, and very much at their own sweet will, throughout the remaining hours of darkness, they continued energetically to pour lead into the hotel.

20
FIRE AND FLAMES

FEELING satisfied that the train was safe, Mr Curnow had made all speed back to Glenrowan, where he found his wife and sister in a state of anxious dread for his safety and their own. Only a few minutes before, a man whom they believed to be Ned Kelly had come to the house; but it proved to be a stranger just arrived in Glenrowan, and the return of Mr Curnow relieved them of their greatest fear. Hiding away the scarf and his clothes, which were soaked with dew from the long grass, the schoolmaster went to bed, telling the others to do the same, so that if the outlaws came they should have no proof against him of having warned the police. When the sound of the firing began he dressed himself hastily and went over to learn the news, but was ordered by the police to return to his house. Up to this time, while Curnow and Bracken had won credit for themselves, the police had done nothing in particular to forfeit it. When the shooting began, though women and children suffered, ignorance justified the fierce firing, and the attacking party were not to blame. From this time onward almost nothing was done which any member of the force engaged can look back upon with bare satisfaction, let alone with pride. An entire absence from foolish rashness is the only commendable quality of which the police gave evidence that day, and this was shown to such as strikingly unheroic degree that people smiled cynically when commending it.

Matters had begun well enough with the spirited rush by Mr Hare and his constables, but that charge has either begun in heedlessness, or it stopped too soon. If Mr Hare's object was to avoid possible loss of life and merely prevent the outlaws' escape, he might have disposed his men so as to surround the house and shut up the enemy within it. If, on the other hand, his intention was to take the hotel by assault, one is surprised that he was checked in this bold design by a mere shot in the wrist. The odds against the outlaws were four to one. With the exception of himself, not a man of his force was wounded by the first volleys, and a determined rush upon the house would have secured it, putting an end one could contemplate with satisfaction to the bushrangers' long career.

But if the first attack was badly advised or half-heartedly executed, it was heroism itself compared with what followed. Knowing that non-combatants were in the house, the police, firing more or less from shelter, continued to pitilessly riddle it with shot, and in the early discharges one of Mrs Jones' children was mortally wounded. Another, a girl of fifteen or sixteen, had been particularly friendly with the Kellys, as had been also her mother, and the latter must have cursed the impulse which had made her detain the prisoners for Ned Kelly's interrupted lecture. Now, she turned upon them fiercely, denouncing them as curs for not leaving the house and fighting in the open, while she also heaped frantic curses upon the police when after the first discharge her little boy was heard screaming piteously in the pitch-dark room where he lay.

Everyone longed to escape, but between fear of the outlaws and the police no one dared make a move. Presently the firing slackened, and Miss Jones walked into the big dark room where the prisoners crouched close together on the floor, and speaking with orders from the Kellys, she said, "All women and children are to leave the house."

Immediately there was a rush of sobbing women and children into the open air, and their appearance was the signal from renewed firing from the police. A challenge came from someone, "Who goes there?" and, in spite of the answer, "Women and children," the shots still continued. Mrs Jones' little boy was taken out by a man who carried him in his arms. Miss Jones was wounded in making her escape, but she and many others reached a place of safety with their lives. The plate-layer, Reardon, and his wife were delayed in their exit from the hotel, for they had to wait for one of the children, whose limbs were cramped from lying beneath a bed for safety, and they were all driven back to the hotel by the hotness of the fire which met them as they sallied into the open and approached the police lines.

This firing upon women and children, even in the darkness and the first confusion of the fight, was bad enough, but far more shameful is the fact that it continued after day had broken and more police had arrived on the scene, so that forces were ample to checkmate any possible move by the outlaws. It was daylight, or almost daylight, when the Reardon family made their second attempt to leave the house. Dan Kelly had given them permission, but said they would all be shot by the police. Dan Kelly has always regarded as a cruel and bloodthirsty villain, who took a pleasure in killing for its own sake, and, on former occasions victims of the gang's exploits certainly believed that they owed their lives simply to Dan's fear of his elder brother. But here at least, to do him justice, he showed more manly spirit. According to Mrs Reardon, he spoke to her a little before she left the house for the second time. "If you escape", he said, "see Hare and tell him not to let his men fire any more till daylight, so that all these people may go in safety. When the house is empty, we will fight for ourselves."

Mr Hare was then wounded, and Mrs Reardon had again to face the undisciplined police fire. This time she escaped from the ferocious friends of order. A sergeant of police, in spite of her screams of mercy, fired directly at her as she ran, and afterwards she showed bullet holes in the cloak with which she wrapped her baby. Her son begged her to go back, crying that she would be shot, but she refused, saying that it would be just as well to die in the open as in the house, and ultimately she reached the police lines unhurt. Her husband and her son, however, were less fortunate, being driven again to the house, the later receiving a bullet wound in the back as he crawled upon the ground for safety. The senseless ferocity of the police would be hard to believe if it were not confirmed from evidence even among themselves, one constable swearing that he saw Mrs Reardon deliberately fired at, and that he himself threatened to shoot the man who did it should he fire again. Though normally a brave and cool-headed officer, Mrs Reardon's assailant like others had been worked up to such a stage of pitiable excitement that he seemed not to know what he was doing.

A Tall Grotesque Figure.

During this time the outlaws were only occasionally returning the police fire, and the prisoners in the dark house with them knew little of what they were doing. They were clad in their armour, during at least a part of that time, and now and then the prisoners heard the sound of bullets ringing upon it. While this armour, made by some local blacksmith, with huge headpieces quilted inside, probably by the Kelly's sisters, gave the outlaws comparative safety on the head, chest, back, and sides which it covered, it nevertheless largely helped to their destruction. Each suit, made of ¼-in. iron plates, weighed nearly 100 pounds. Unhampered by armour, the Kellys might at the last minute have made a bolt for liberty, and at any rate would have shot down some of their assailants; but encased in iron they could scarcely move and could not hold their rifles to their shoulders to take aim.

It is hard to know what their plans were. Their horses were tethered to trees near the hotel, and probably they meant to mount and ride away, but early in the fight these horses were discovered by the police and shot to prevent the outlaws' escape. They, however, could scarcely have known this, and the three other members of the gang were probably waiting anxiously and without a leader for the return of Ned, who disappeared from the house into the darkness after the first volleys had been fired. What he went for, no one knows. Escape, at least alone, cannot have been his object, for at eight o'clock he was seen among the trees, a tall, grotesque figure, stalking towards the hotel and firing with his revolver on the police. His blood-stained rifle had been found in the grass not long before. A wound in the hand made it useless to him, and now with a revolver only he faced the nine police who fired on him as he tried to regain the hotel. Under a long grey overcoat he wore his armour, and though he staggered beneath the blows from rifle bullets which struck him again and again, he tapped his armour-clad breast and laughed derisively. Then they fired at his legs. He wore no armour there, and presently he fell. The police, headed by Sergeant Steele, rushed in and secured him, wrenching away his revolver. With many wounds in his arms and legs he lay helplessly cursing upon the ground. His career as an outlaw over forever, he was presently stripped of his armour and carried to the railway station where a doctor attended to his wounds.

Before Ned Kelly was taken, Superintendent Sadlier had arrived from Benalla, and from his coming there was more semblance of order and decency in the proceedings. Firing upon the building still continued, but the order was given to fire high, which it was supposed would prevent the outlaws leaving the house or standing up unharmed to shoot, while sparing any non- combatants who might be lying on the floor; but of course it rendered escape very dangerous to the unfortunate prisoners still confined.

Nevertheless, at intervals a few left the building, and at ten o'clock, when Mr Sadlier ordered a complete cessation of firing for ten minutes and called upon those remaining to come out, with the exception of a man named Cherry, who lay mortally wounded in a detached building, they all did so. From the escapees' report, it appeared that Joe Byrne was dead, shot in the groin, and that Dan Kelly and Steve Hart were still alive. Repeated appeals were made to them to surrender, but without effect, and numbers of the police begged Mr Sadlier to let them rush the building. This request Mr Sadlier constantly refused, at this stage perhaps with reason, as life would probably have been lost, and now there was no longer good cause to refrain from pouring volleys into the hotel and shooting the outlaws without danger to police and private citizens.

During the fight, if so it can be called, the press representatives were every few minutes sending away sensational bulletins to their respective journals in Melbourne, where the excitement caused by the affair at Glenrowan was intense. Police officers and public grew somewhat hysterical. The day was passing, and though shots came seldom, if ever, from the building, it was feared the outlaws might yet escape if they remained uncaptured when darkness came on. Mr Sadlier was induced to telegraph to Melbourne for a cannon, and with a force of artillerymen a 12-pounder Armstrong gun actually started by train for Glenrowan. The Government astronomer was asked if he could send up an electric light plant in case the siege should continue until night. It would be scarcely practicable in the time, he said, whereupon the Chief Secretary, Mr Ramsay, wired to Mr Sadlier suggesting the building of huge bonfires to light up the scene, and also recommending the construction of a great wooden shield, under cover of which the police might approach the hotel in safety.

None of these devices were, however, needed, and the cannon returned from Seymour without firing a shot, for at about three o'clock in the afternoon Senior Constable Johnston offered to set alight to the building. After consultation with Mr O'Connor and others Mr Sadlier consented. Kate Kelly and Mrs Skillion, who with numerous other sympathisers had come upon the scene, were riding about dressed in their best watching the siege, and after it was decided to fire the house Mrs Skillion wished to enter and see her brother, but Mr Sadlier refused as the fire might not have taken, and another non-combatant in the house would have put fresh difficulties in the way of the attack. Mrs Skillion, indeed, was quite capable of deliberately remaining with her brother and taking up a rifle to assist the defenders.

All things being ready, under cover of a heavy fire upon the windows from the police, Johnston ran forward and fired the building. In a very few minutes the place was in flames. Kate Kelly looked on, piteously crying, "Oh, my poor brother! My poor brother!" The Reverend Dean Gibney, a Roman Catholic Clergyman, gallantly rushed towards the burning building. There might be wounded men within to be saved, or dying ones to whom he could give the last comforts of their religion. Mr Sadlier tried to prevent him, but could not do so, and there was then a general rush for the hotel. From an outbuilding was removed the wounded man, Martin Cherry; from the house the body of Joe Byrne. The bodies of Dan Kelly and Steve Hart were seen by Dean Gibney, lying side by side in another part of the house. They did not wear their armour, which was, however, near them, and it may be that they shot one another rather than be taken; but the manner of their death was never known, for all of them that was ever seen again was some charred remains, discovered in the smouldering ruins of the hotel. These remains Mr Sadlier handed over to their friends for burial, while the body of Joe Byrne was taken to Benalla, where at the magisterial enquiry it was found that he was shot as an outlaw. With Joe Byrne's body to Benalla there went that of Martin Cherry, an innocent victim of the fight, who died shortly after his removal from the hotel, while later, in the Wangaratta hospital, Mrs Jones' little boy died of his wounds.

Over fifty police had taken part in the fight. It was not an heroic combat, and the work was sadly botched and bungled, with much resultant misery to innocent people. Still, three of the outlaws were dead, the fourth was wounded and awaiting his trial. The pestilent Kelly gang could trouble Victoria no more, and congratulatory telegrams to the officers concerned and to the Victorian Government flashed over the wires one after another from every corner of Australia.

NED KELLY'S ARMOUR. FROM A SKETCH MADE BY MR. T. CARRINGTON.
1—THE HELMET, FRONT VIEW. 2—SIDE VIEW OF HELMET. 3—BREASTPLATE. 4—BACK PLATE. 5—BACK LAPPET.
6—FRONT VIEW OF ARMOUR.

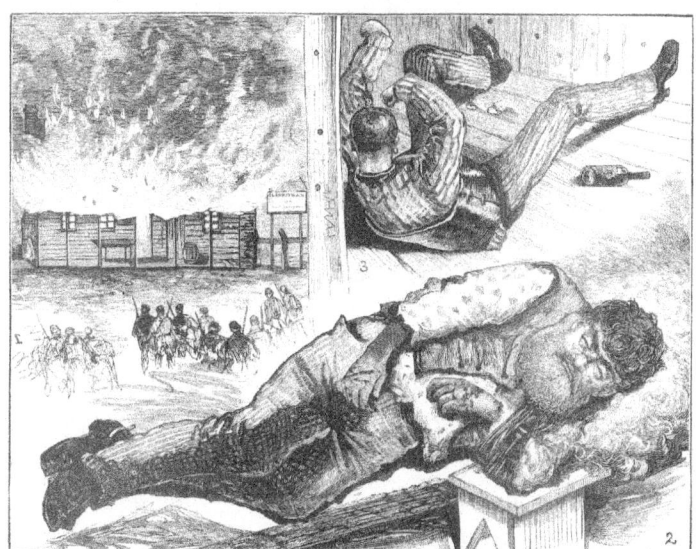

DESTRUCTION OF THE KELLY GANG. DRAWN BY MR. T. CARRINGTON DURING THE ENCOUNTER.
1—SETTING FIRE TO GLENROWAN HOTEL 2—NED KELLY LYING ON BUNK IN STATION-MASTER'S HOUSE. 3—SCENE THROUGH THE DOOR OF THE INN, BYRNE LYING DEAD ON THE FLOOR WHERE HE FELL JUST IN FRONT OF THE BAR.

21
THE LAST OF THE BUSHRANGERS

WITH three of their number dead and the fourth a prisoner, the career of the Kelly gang ended once and for all on the day the hotel at Glenrowan, riddled like a sieve with police bullets, went up in flames, but for months afterwards the sympathisers remained in sullen, threatening mood, and while Ned Kelly lived the gang and their exploits were a constant topic of thought and conversation all through the country.

In the final stages of the Kelly drama events moved quickly, and changing emotions rapidly succeeded one another in the minds of law-abiding citizens.

The horror occasioned by Sherritt's cold-blooded murder was followed by intense excitement and eager expectation when news came that the outlaws were surrounded at Glenrowan. Excitement gave place to relief as hope was converted into the certainty that the Kelly gang was no more, and afterwards with reflection there came somewhat contemptuous regret for the unheroic part that circumstances had forced upon the police in the affair. They did their duty in the main, and Superintendent Sadlier was undoubtedly right in determining that the lives of none of his constables should be avoidably sacrificed, but the shooting of innocent civilians was hard to explain away or forgive, and to friends of law and order the story of Glenrowan was scarcely more a source of satisfaction than of shame. To the Kelly sympathisers the gang not unnaturally became more than ever heroes with their death, and over the charred remains of Hart and Dan Kelly, which were given to their relatives, a wake was held at the residence of Mrs Skillion, whereat fierce vows of vengeance were registered. The fire had rendered the bodies unrecognisable and no one was able to see by what wounds they met their death; but the popular theory was that, finding the case hopeless, they had taken off their armour and shot one another to prevent falling into the hands of the police. Reardon, the plate-layer, and other witnesses, who had heard Hart and Dan Kelly conversing together in the hotel, were convinced that this was the case, but Ned Kelly, when asked his opinion, said he believed they were too cowardly to voluntarily accept death.

As for Ned himself, his plight was worse than that of his associates, for they at least had the satisfaction of dying in fight, while he was a humiliated prisoner, with almost certain death in prospect. His wounds were dressed as well as possible, and for one night he remained in the lock-up at Benalla where he was interviewed by McIntyre and others of the police, and on the following day he was conveyed by the ordinary train from the North-East to Melbourne. His expected arrival created extraordinary excitement in the city, with the result that extraordinary precautions were taken to prevent any rioting or disorder among the inquisitive crowd which thronged all approaches to the railway station at Spencer-street when the train was due. Elaborate barriers had been erected near the station entrance where uniformed police paraded, but all this demonstration was a mere hoax which successfully deluded the people. The train in which Kelly travelled pulled up at North Melbourne, the station next adjoining Spencer-street, and a few plain-clothes police and detectives, who had unostentatiously strolled on to the platform, immediately approached the brake van containing the wounded bushranger and his armed guards. He was quickly carried to a vehicle which was in waiting, with a mattress on the floor, and driven away to the Melbourne Gaol where a bed in the Gaol hospital awaited him. He was, indeed, in a pitiable state, suffering greatly from his wounds, while his face was covered with livid bruises made by concussion with the iron helmet when it was struck by the numerous bullets from the police rifles, which flattened themselves against it. As the bushranger was carried to the prison van a murmur of pity arose from the few spectators, some of whom doubtless had their own grudges against the law, while others merely felt involuntary compassion for a man helpless and fallen, ruffian though they recognised him to be.

Mr O'Connor and his black trackers, and Mr Hare, wounded like Ned Kelly, were also passengers by the train which took the outlaw to Melbourne, and Mr Hare had a good reception at Spencer-street, where he was met by the late Sir W. J. (then Mr) Clarke and his wife, who drove him in their carriage to the police depot at Richmond. For weeks afterwards Mr Hare's wound was attended to by Dr Charles Ryan, a surgeon lately returned from service with the Turkish army in the war against Russia. Dr Ryan sent in his bill of some four hundred and fifty guineas to the Government, who also saw that Ned Kelly's wounds were attended to, though at somewhat less expense by Dr Shields, the Government medical officer at the Melbourne Gaol. Over £600 was spent on surgical attendance upon Mr Hare; but to prove his desire for rigid economy, the Government, as commented on by members of the Royal Commission which enquired into the Kelly outbreak, questioned the payment of four guineas for the treatment of a black tracker wounded in the head at Glenrowan.

In the hospital Ned Kelly gradually recovered from his injuries, but frequent remands were necessary before he was able to appear at the police court at Beechworth, where, ultimately, he was committed to stand his trial for murder. In the meantime, matters were going ill in the police force, in which the smouldering jealousies and bitterness, engendered largely by the Chief Commissioner's favouritism for Mr Hare, broke out into fresh flame, and the public became painfully aware that the affairs of the police department were in a thoroughly disorganised and unsatisfactory condition.

Apart from the chief officers employed in the Kelly business, trouble arose in the lower ranks owing to the unwillingness of certain sergeants and police constables to accept service in the neighbourhood of Greta, since they considered their lives would be in danger from the vengeance of Kelly sympathisers. Black marks were put against the names of one or two of these, a proceeding which, in view of the extraordinary condition of affairs then existing, the Police Commission considered was not warranted.

On August 11, after a hearing extending over many days in the Beechworth Police Court, Ned Kelly was committed for trial on the charge of murdering the police party at Stringy Bark Creek in 1878. Every day the court had been crowded, for though in Beechworth the gang had not many sympathisers, there was great curiosity to see the notorious outlaw and his sisters and other relatives, who were constantly present at the proceedings and who took an affectionate farewell of him when he was ordered for removal to Melbourne Gaol. There he remained until the end of October, when he was put upon his trial before Mr. Justice Barry at the Melbourne Criminal Court. The trial, which created intense interest, was not a very long one, and ended in the only way possible, with a verdict of guilty and sentence of death against the outlaw, who was convicted on evidence largely contributed by himself in his boastful conversation with his prisoners at the sticking up of Faithfull's Creek, and on the evidence of Constable McIntyre, who had been an eyewitness at the murders at Stringy Bark Creek.

Up to and for some time after his conviction, Kelly maintained an unconcerned and even defiant demeanour. He was much in request with pressmen as a subject for interviews, and his vainglorious accounts of exploits which he did not attempt to deny made copy eagerly devoured by thousands of newspaper readers.

Facts were too clearly proved against Kelly to make denial possible, therefore in all his outpourings he attempted to arouse sympathy by representing himself and his family as the victims of wicked police oppression, which had forced him, against his will, to adopt a career of robbery and murder. With a discreditably large proportion of the population his specious appeals for sympathy were successful, and sympathisers, reinforced by many foolish people who weakly allowed feelings of compassion to get the better of their sense of decency and justice, made strong efforts to induce the Government to commute the sentence passed upon the outlaw. All the agitation, however, was in vain; and on November 11 Ned Kelly was hanged in Melbourne Gaol. He met his death with a fair amount of courage, though he could not trust himself to make a speech as he had contemplated doing, and when asked if he wished to say anything immediately before his execution, he contented himself with murmuring, "Ah, well—I suppose it has come to this!"

Some thousands of people, mostly, as the "Argus" phrased it, "of the lower orders," had gathered outside the Gaol at the hour fixed for the execution, and they looked up expectantly as the clock struck ten, in the hope of seeing a black flag hoisted above the Gaol, but they were denied this morbid satisfaction, for the authorities gave no sign of what was occurring within the walls. Kate Kelly, with whom much legitimate sympathy was felt in her trouble, forfeited all claims to it by extraordinary conduct on the day of her brother's execution. Doubtless she had a sincere regard for him, as her courageous assistance to the gang, in defiance of law, had often witnessed; but, stronger than love or grief, was a desire for theatrical display, which had its grimly humorous side. On the afternoon of her brother's execution, dressed in deep black, she held a private reception in a public room hired for the purpose in Melbourne, and allowed those presented to her the privilege of shaking hands to show their sympathy and their sense of her importance, after which they passed on in silence and gave place to others awaiting their turn. About this performance there was, at least, a kind of farcical dignity; but in the evening Kate Kelly sank to lower depths, and gratified morbid curiosity by appearing on the stage of a Melbourne music-hall, at the invitation of an enterprising manager.

In Ned Kelly died the last of the Victorian bushrangers, and with the increase of population and the improved methods of communication, even in the still sparsely populated North- Eastern District, it is scarcely likely that he can ever have a successful imitator. But it was long before the fear of another outbreak of the part of exasperated sympathisers disappeared, and those best informed upon the matter considered the danger greatest. Several references have been made to a Royal Commission which enquired into and reported exhaustively upon necessary reforms in the police administration and all circumstances connected with the Kelly gang's long career. This Commission began its sittings early in 1881, and after sitting for months, during which it heard a vast amount of evidence from members of the police and a great number of civilians, it recommended the retirement upon their superannuation allowances of Captain Standish, Mr Hare, and Mr Nicolson. The Commission considered that the first-named officers were principally to blame for the jealousy and want of esprit-de-corps which they found existing in the force; but Mr Nicolson and Mr Sadlier they also blamed for errors of judgement in connection with the pursuit of the Kellys, and, in fact, though the Commissioners had a word of praise for most of the officers upon some points, blame was far more freely bestowed than praise in their report.

Upon the best means of copying with lawlessness in the North-Eastern District, and the anticipated outbreak of Kelly sympathisers, the Commission took evidence with closed doors, from witnesses familiar with the country and its inhabitants. Under the new head of the police force, Mr H. M. Chomley, who was appointed Acting Chief Commissioner during the progress of the enquiry and afterwards confirmed in the position, measures in accordance with the recommendations from various sources, and approved by the Commission, were taken to secure the tranquillity of the district. The Lands Department allied itself with the Police Department in promoting order by refusing to grant land in the district to any applicant who received a bad character from the police, and the knowledge that the mounted constables, by an adverse report, could prevent them from obtaining coveted selections, had a most salutary effect upon a number of the inhabitants. At the same time efforts were made to get new blood into the district by inducing a good class of men to take up land, and these efforts were largely successful.

Finally, new police stations were established at commanding points where mischief might be apprehended; the troopers were armed with regulation weapons and better horsed than formerly, and special endeavours were made to secure an active, intelligent class of men who would constantly ride about the country, keeping in touch with one another and with the inhabitants of every type.

These endeavours have been eminently successful; and at the present day—though horses and cattle may occasionally strangely change brands and ownership in the hills—life and property are on the whole as safe in the once notorious Kelly district as in any other part of Victoria.

www.ingramcontent.com/pod-product-compliance
Lightning Source LLC
Chambersburg PA
CBHW030943090426
42737CB00007B/515